Lenny Kravitz

The Life The Genius The Legend

James Court

NEW HAVEN PUBLISHING

Published 2019
New Haven Publishing Ltd
www.newhavenpublishingltd.com
newhavenpublishing@gmail.com

Front cover image © dpa picture alliance/Alamy
Back cover image © Benédicte Thibaudat

newhaven
publishing

For Sam, Charlie and Danny

Thank you to Annso Dubreuil and all
the team at LKonline, Frenchboard,
for providing the photography in this book.

Bruno Tachon
Bénédicte Thibaudat
Laurent Valay
Romain Pasquini
Vanessa Favaretto
Chrystelle Roujean

Content

The Writing on the Wall

The Life: The period between birth and death, or the experience or state of being alive.

The Genius: Exceptional intellectual or creative power or other natural ability. Exceptionally intelligent person or one with exceptional skill in a particular area of activity. Very clever or ingenious.

The Legend: Someone very famous and admired, usually because of their ability in a particular area.

Most established rock stars have a somewhat challenging upbringing; they have a back story that drove them to escape the perceived mundane repetition of everyday life. There is usually something in their childhood that pushed them in a new direction, a direction to pursue excitement and something different. Commonly it's something that drove them to stardom, or at the very least to seek it - something in their early life motivated them to seek an alternative; more often than not something, or someone, inspired them. It could be a broken home, for example, or abject poverty, a rags to riches story that led towards seeking a more appealing, exhilarating and stimulating occupation... that occupation being a 'Rock Star'.

Leonard Kravitz, however, had a more privileged upbringing than the standard wannabe rock or pop star; his compulsion to become a famous musician was more born out of pure ambition and desire than any sort of escape from a current lifestyle. He was motivated by his surroundings and musical upbringing, being exposed to some of the greats of all time from a young age. This was both from a fan point of view and, more importantly, from a personal one. He even stated later on that he never really wanted fame itself but simply wanted to be a musician; it was the art and the creative process that was the driver, and this initial early motivation came from his parents.

Lenny's mother was actress Roxie Albertha Roker. She was born on August 28th 1929. She played, amongst many other roles, Helen Willis on the popular CBS sitcom *The Jeffersons*, appearing on the show for ten years from 1975 to 1985. At this time she was part of what was widely reported and acknowledged as the first interracial couple actually shown on mainstream television in the US; she played the part alongside Franklin Edward Cover, who played Tom Willis. She was born in Miami but grew up in Brooklyn, New York. As well as this high-profile role she had a distinguished career, becoming a successful stage actress, and she starred in many movies from 1974 through to 1990.

His father, Seymour Kravitz, later shortened to Sy Kravitz, was born on December 10th 1924 in Brooklyn, New York City. He joined the military when he was young and became a Green Beret; his brother Leonard Kravitz followed him into the military but was tragically killed in action in the Korean War at just 19 years of age. His death however was heroic as, during a Chinese attack, he reportedly saved his entire platoon. His actions earned him the Distinguished Service Cross, but controversially not the Medal of Honor. Later in 2014 this contentious decision was reevaluated and correctly revoked and he was awarded the Medal of Honor alongside 23 other servicemen. It came to light that the original contemptuous decision to deny him the distinguished Medal of Honor was because of ancestry and heritage and eventually a verdict correctly amended this. Sy Kravitz himself was of Ukrainian and Jewish heritage and went on to become an established filmmaker and producer of newsreels, as well as being involved in the music industry. He worked on the US channel NBC. In 1963 Sy married Roxie Roker and a year later on 26th May 1964 the successful celebrity couple had their first and only child, who they named after his war hero uncle, Leonard Albert Kravitz.

Lenny's parents, being successful in the world of celebrity and television, both had busy schedules and so early on in his childhood Lenny had a sort of split routine. He would spend weekdays in the affluent area on the upper east side of the city with his parents and weekends would be spent at his grandmother's house in the Bedford-Stuyvesant neighbourhood of Brooklyn, a much less wealthy area by comparison. Lenny attended P.S. 6 elementary school situated on Staten Island. Lenny loved his grandparents and in particular his grandfather, who he was extremely close to. His grandfather was young for his age: he would go running, he would go swimming, he would cycle for miles and he would hang around with younger people. Lenny recalled that even at age 90 his grandfather learned to roller-skate, such was his love for activity, and would spend hours at a time at the rink. He later described his grandfather as, simply, 'a very cool guy'.

Because of his work Lenny's father introduced and exposed the youngster to music frequently during Lenny's early life. As well as his TV work Sy Kravitz also worked as a jazz promoter, working freelance, and so Lenny was introduced from an early age to jazz, and rhythm and blues. He soon became absorbed in music and from the age of five he wanted to become a musician of some sort. His parents were extremely supportive of his love for music and took Lenny to shows whenever they could. Lenny saw James Brown at The Apollo Theatre and The Jackson 5 when he was six years old at Madison Square Garden; Lenny still has a photograph on his wall in a gold frame in his house in Paris that was taken on 16 July 1971 by his father and shows the Jackson 5 onstage at Madison Square Garden. It was the first show little Lenny ever attended and he was mesmerised by it. Ironically it would be Michael himself taking instructions from Lenny in the years ahead. This was one of many shows and performances he was exposed to, linked to his parents' celebrity and musical connections. Another key figure Lenny was very close to was Sid Bernstein, who became a sort of godfather figure to him. Working as a booking agent through the 1960s Sid Bernstein was a large architect for the infamous musical British Invasion during this time; he was widely credited with bringing The Beatles to the US after reading about the group in the UK press. He also brought over The Rolling Stones, The Moody Blues, Hermans Hermits and The

Kinks. He later organised many concerts for some of the biggest names in popular music and must have had a wealth of knowledge to pass on to the youngster fast becoming engrossed in the concerts and shows surrounding his parents and their influential friends.

Lenny's father became a notable figure in music because of his freelance work. He became friends with many of the big jazz acts of the day including Bobby Short, Ella Fitzgerald, Sarah Vaughan, Miles Davis and Duke Ellington who even played 'Happy Birthday' for Lenny when he was five. He was also exposed to soul, including James Brown, Aretha Franklin, Al Green, Stevie Wonder, Curtis Mayfield, and Gladys Knight. All the above would be key influences in Lenny's sound going forward. Lenny would also frequently visit the theatre where his mother worked and was actively encouraged by her to pursue his ambitions and dreams in music. It's no wonder with such exposure to music and performing, and being surrounded by such prominent and guiding figures, that the young Lenny would have developed an appetite for his own musical future.

It wasn't long before Lenny started playing music himself, first learning acoustic guitar and then the piano which was situated in the family apartment. When Lenny was eleven years old the family moved from New York to Los Angeles when his mother landed her role in *The Jeffersons*. Here the young aspiring musician was exposed to the West Coast music scene, which was totally different to what the young Lenny was used to. He also had his first taste of performing when his mother got him an audition for a boys' choir, which he passed. This however was not just a small backstreet church choir, this was the California Boys Choir and it was something of significance. The California Boys Choir at this time was rated as the second highest boys' choir in the world, only falling behind The Vienna Boys Choir in Austria. This meant that Lenny rehearsed every day as part of the commitment: the day would start at around 8am and there were theory classes, harmony classes and various staging classes and it became a major focus in his life - it was in essence a full musical commitment for any youngster in the choir. The choir held a major performance at The Hollywood Bowl, the famous amphitheatre in the Hollywood Hills, giving Lenny an early exposure to a major event. Whilst in

10

the choir he continued with teaching himself guitar, bass, drums and keyboards, now fast becoming a mini multi-instrumentalist, and he even starred in several TV commercials through his mother's influence.

Musically, whereas New York had exposed Lenny to mostly soul, R&B and jazz, moving to Santa Monica brought a different music scene altogether. Here during 1975 he discovered Led Zeppelin, Jimi Hendrix, Cream and The Who. He also became a huge Kiss fan and loved the harder edge rock sounds that these bands provided. At just 11 Lenny had been surrounded already by established serious jazz acts and promoters, and had celebrity parents. He was now discovering and becoming captivated by a totally different musical culture, that of rock. The above mix of musical influences, from the jazz and R&B of New York to the rock element in LA, gave Lenny a huge catalogue of styles that he wanted to play. Later, when he searched for a record deal, he recalled that because of his broad musical awareness it was difficult for him to stick within one genre; the mixture of all the musical styles he was exposed to as a youngster gave him a wide repertoire, and therefore made him difficult to pigeonhole into a specific area of music. It's interesting on reflection that the very thing that made Lenny Kravitz unique in his sound, that of a musical blend of all the early influences he was exposed to, rock, funk, psychedelia, soul and jazz, was the very thing that hindered him initially in getting a record deal. He was basically too talented to place somewhere convenient.

A record company will immediately want to place you somewhere within the industry: jazz, soul, rock or pop for example. In addition, Lenny was seen as a 'black artist' and so immediately was in a separate genre altogether. Only when black artists reached a certain threshold would there be a cross over into 'mainstream charts' and at the time when Lenny was searching for a record deal this was not an everyday occurrence. If you're playing everything in a variety of styles, and visually you're immediately seen as a black artist, it's a problem, especially for an unknown unestablished act.

At high school Lenny recalled not being part of any particular group. There were, as expected within a high school environment, certain groups that hung out together. Lenny however was never part of any one group but was happy hanging out with all of them equally, and he was accepted by them all. His background of having a white father and a black mother and being exposed to many different styles and influences gave him a free and open attitude to all around him - everything and everyone was happily tolerated and he never stuck to one particular area, which reflected his upbringing and receptiveness to others. Lenny recalled having to fill a form in at school that required a tick in a box on ethnicity - white, black, Asian etc - and having a black mother and a white father Lenny said he paused at the question, not knowing what to tick. He was told to tick 'black' and for the first time he said he felt pigeonholed, and he wondered why the box itself was even relevant. Attending high school at the same time as Lenny was Saul Hudson, and Lenny recalled being friends with Saul but not really becoming too close. Saul would later be renamed Slash and would co-write with Lenny, as well as becoming one of the most famous rock guitarists on the planet. Lenny was re-acquainted with Slash at an awards ceremony and the two realised they were in fact high school friends; it was because of this that they later collaborated on Lenny's second album *Mama Said*.

Lenny now started progressing with his musical ambitions and, alongside the piano and guitar, started learning drums and bass. The drums in particular were a favourite; he had always wanted to be a drummer but as his parents had an apartment in New York previously this clearly was not an option. Now in LA Lenny started to develop fast on drums as well as bass, guitar and piano.

After graduating from high school Lenny left home and, influenced by his past, followed his dream of becoming a musician. He was now immersed in music and fast becoming a fully-fledged young songwriter and multi-instrumentalist. Lenny decided to search out record companies who would perhaps be interested in the songs that he had written so far. He was at this time heavily influenced by David Bowie and decided on changing his performing name to Romeo Blue. Bowie however was not the only influence that Lenny had: another up and coming multi-instrumentalist really captured his attention and became a major imprint on him and his approach to music.

Prince had just released his second album and in particular the song 'I Wanna Be Your Lover', which caught Lenny's attention. It was however his third album *Dirty Mind*, released a year later in 1980, which really had an impact, and Lenny loved it. Not only did he love the music, the 16-year-old loved the attitude and was completely taken in with the sound and the imagery. Lenny saw a similar background in Prince: he saw a multi-instrumentalist, someone playing every note on an album, someone playing guitar the way he wanted to. He immediately identified with Prince and the influence he had on the early Romeo Blue was huge, and shaped his outlook as he further crafted his songs, image and sound. Prince and Lenny would go on to be great friends in the years ahead.

Another key figure that had an influence often later attributed to Lenny's work was John Lennon. He was assassinated in New York on 8th December 1980 and naturally the music world stood still. Lenny's early work, and indeed many of his future songs, had the feeling of Lennon, particularly in the hippie, we are all one/ love is all you need/ let love rule influence. Lennon, during the first few months of 1981, was naturally brought to the attention of every aspiring musician in the world, and in particular those who were in New York. It's no coincidence that some of Lennon's imprint and significance would work their way into some of Lenny's early work and beyond into the future.

Lenny continued writing and recording tracks that would eventually find their way onto his first album; for now though the ideas were developing into various songs. He initially wanted a fully-fledged band with him in the studio but at the time couldn't afford to pay seasoned musicians for their time. In addition, the players whom he could afford were not good enough to play what he wanted them to play, or more to the point they couldn't get the sound Lenny wanted. The conclusion was a simple one and shaped the way Lenny would record his music for the next thirty or so years. A friend suggested to him to do it all himself. Being influenced heavily by Prince, this was a logical conclusion, and Lenny followed this path. Recording drums first, while trying to sing the song in his head, was one method, while another was for his engineer at the time, Henry Hirsch, to play the keyboards alongside Lenny on the drums so he had a guide to follow. He would then erase the keyboards so the drums remained clean on the track and start over. Lenny would then put down guitar, bass, percussion and so on to build the track.

At this time Lenny also became a session musician, lending out his talents to anyone who was looking to create a demo tape, and he quickly became the 'go to guy' for anyone looking for a session musician who could play a variety of instruments. This meant he worked increasingly alongside keyboardist and bass player Henry Hirsch and the two became more collaborative and started composing some original material together.

Henry Hirsch would go on to be a major collaborator and engineer alongside Lenny. They initially met as far back as 1985 and kept in touch, loosely collaborating from time to time. The partnership they had would continue for more than twenty years, and still continues to this day. Lenny started to book himself more sessions alongside Henry Hirsch's at the studio and this soon turned into Lenny playing all instruments with Hirsch engineering and assisting where needed. It was from here on the two became strong collaborators and continued writing and recording together going forward.

The pair now started to work more on developing the sound to the songs Lenny had previously written. It wasn't long before the partnership had come good and now, armed with demos, they decided it was the right time to search out a record deal. They both had an interest in vintage instruments, and used them wherever they could; anything that would give something more characteristic and distinctive to the sound was used. They had strength in Lenny's writing ability, which of course was strong, but they hoped that the instruments and studio techniques would elevate the sound of the recordings, a sound that they hoped would give them that point of difference to other sounds of the day. However, Lenny's aforementioned influences, of various different styles, had made their way to his sound and he was seen, initially, as a sort of an 'impersonation' of styles rather than an individual with his own sound. He was told in no uncertain terms that he

14

needed to change his sound and style to enable a record company to back him. The record companies wanted to immediately pigeonhole him into the black music scene and for this Lenny, or Romeo Blue, was required to change.

Disappointed at his initial rejections the aspiring Romeo Blue headed back to the East Coast still in pursuit of his record deal and determined to land the contract he yearned for. It was now that he decided Romeo Blue was not the future and went back to his original name. All was not lost however for the young aspiring musician as his personal life was about to become interesting as he met, and fell in love with, a young aspiring actress.

Lisa Bonet was born in San Francisco, California. Her father was born in Texas and is of African American descent while her mother, a music teacher, was half Jewish. She recalled on meeting Lenny that when they both discovered that they had a parent who was Jewish -Lenny's father and Lisa's mother - she felt a connection to him and opened up a lot more than she had with anyone she had met previously. Lenny said after that he felt that Lisa was the female equivalent of him, almost like a twin; he saw himself in her. She was the catalyst for him to start writing, and the writing was brutally honest. He wanted to be real to himself and have this come through in his songs. Lenny wanted to make a difference and felt he had something to say through his music. The two became very close and later, on November 16th 1987, they were married on Lisa's 20th birthday. They then settled back in New York to continue their lives together, Lisa as the aspiring actress and Lenny the aspiring musician.

Continuing on with the writing and development of what would be his first album Lenny wrote a significant song that would eventually be the title track of his first album, 'Let Love Rule'. At this time Lenny and Lisa, in 1987, were living in a rented loft on Broome street in New York, the couple renting it from a guy who used to play with Bob Marley. It was while living in this area of the city that Lenny drew inspiration. There were squatters and regular robberies, many at knifepoint, and this gave the heavily dreadlocked Lenny a hippie perspective which showed in his writing and songs during this period. He was living a type of bohemian non-conformist life, pursuing his ambitions of a record contract and stardom, along with many others in the area. With no record label behind him Lenny was forced to record his songs in a cheap run-down studio in Hoboken situated in New Jersey on the Hudson River. The area boasts a great view of the Manhattan skyline as an inspirational background for any aspiring musician or writer. On returning to the loft one day after a recording session Lenny wrote on the wall 'Let Love Rule'; he later said it was something he just thought of and, on passing the newly penned wall art every day, picked up his guitar and wrote the song. There was something about what he wrote on the wall that drew him, and as he saw it every day it worked its way into his mind. This formed the backdrop to his album and gave a clear guide as to how it should form. The social surroundings Lenny was living in and the 'Let Love Rule' wall art gave Lenny hope and inspiration for the writing on the album - it gave a direction, a guidance, and maybe for the first time it gave him a coherent narrative to the songs. It was time to once again pitch himself to record companies. The writing was on the wall…

Now with a full album completed, Lenny put himself forward again. Once more he was left disappointed as they couldn't feel what he was doing or see any unique potential in him. He again had to sit and listen to record companies battle with what they were listening to: he simply did not fit neatly and snugly within a certain musical area.

In the early 1980s black artists were categorised as just that, a black artist, and they remained in the then 'black charts', but this was changing. There was a cross over coming through and certain artists were pushing this change with their popularity. On record sales this meant that on reaching a certain threshold the artist would cross over into the Billboard Hot 100, as well as being in their own categorised charts. Another change was coming however, especially around other media, which helped record sales, in particular music videos and the introduction of Music Television, or MTV. MTV was a joint venture between American Express and Warner Communications. It made its first appearance in August 1981 but by 1983 it had an audience of around 15 million and was growing rapidly. Music videos were becoming a vital part of any artist's repertoire and were beginning to be seen as an essential part of promotion. MTV targeted the mid 20s generation, who were being abandoned by radio stations. It was, until this point, a rock and roll medium leaning toward white acts and black artists were very much the minority. It was only the crossover of artists like Prince and Michael Jackson that paved the way for Whitney Houston, Lionel Richie, Tina Turner and Janet Jackson, and this kept this crossover going. This crossover held its own until mainstream rap acts emerged in the late 80s and became a regular feature for black artists. A small intervention by MTV in 1982 added the videos for Prince from his album *1999* to its playlist: 'Little Red Corvette' and '1999' itself. It also added videos by Michael Jackson, who was fast becoming the leader in music video, turning them into mini films with choreographed routines. Artists like Michael and Prince instantly became mainstream even though before this exposure they were seen as predominantly black artists. MTV immediately added a new audience and opened up a significant amount of exposure they would not ordinarily have had. Without this it is fair to say it may have taken years of continuous touring to reach this level of exposure. The albums that had singles on the MTV playlist started to accelerate up the charts, and audiences grew rapidly. Record companies were now not just categorising artists on appearance but were looking at whether they had someone with the potential to cross over to the mainstream, someone with the skill and musical ability to do so, someone like Lenny Kravitz…

Eventually, and significantly, an A&R person at Virgin records agreed to give Lenny a short five-minute meeting. A&R, or Artists and Repertoire, is a division of a record label or music publishing company. They are ultimately responsible for talent scouting and overseeing the artistic development of recording artists and songwriters. The amount of time they are willing to give an artist, to meet and review what they have, depends on how interested they are. Lenny was given just a five-minute slot.

A female representative met with Lenny and popped in the cassette. After five minutes she left the room and returned with the then president of Virgin. A deal was offered there and then, the president saying that he saw in Lenny 'Prince meets John Lennon', not a bad comparison. Naturally wind broke of the deal on the record label circuit and the labels that previously dismissed Lenny returned with counter offers. Lenny however was interested in growth and development and felt that Virgin best allowed for this. He was staying, and his deal with Virgin was completed.

In addition to the achievement of finally securing a record deal there was another moment of happiness for Lenny and Lisa when she gave birth to their daughter Zoë Isabella on December 1st 1988. Things were now lined up perfectly for Lenny: his family was complete and he had the record deal he had been hoping to achieve for so long. As the new year came around to 1989, and preparations continued for his debut album, things were looking good...

Lenny Kravitz was now ready to go, and was *sitting on top of the world*.

Photo © Romain Pasquini

Photo © Bruno Tachon

All Aboard the Freedom Train...

Now with his record deal completed Lenny continued with final touches to what would be his debut album. The first single for the album was agreed to be the title track itself, 'Let Love Rule'. The single was released on July 23 1989 and had additional tracks available through the CD EP or 12" single. These were lifted album tracks and were made available on a 4-disc set comprising of 'Let Love Rule', 'Empty Hands' 'Blues for Sister Someone' and 'Flower Child'. The shorter version or 7" single contained just the one B-side of 'Empty Hands'. The video Lenny recorded for the lead single 'Let Love Rule' was nominated for an MTV Video Music Award for best new artist. The video shows Lenny playing in a field with various children walking around holding hands. The footage is very cinematic and shows Lenny playing guitar with his band, interspersed with footage of him playing with the children. The single itself reached number 23 on the mainstream rock tracks chart and number 5 on the modern rock chart with the album itself eventually released two months later on September 19th 1989 with 10 tracks finally selected. His wife Lisa wrote the lyrics for 'Fear' and co-wrote lyrics for 'Rosemary'; other than that *Let Love Rule* is purely a one-man band introducing Lenny Kravitz to the music world.

When Lenny was laying down the drum track for 'Fear' he broke a drumstick, which flew into his eye and injured his cornea. Lenny didn't stop playing and was only rushed to the emergency room once he'd finished. On the CD version - remember this is 1989 - bonus tracks were added: 'Blues for Sister Someone', 'Empty Hands' and 'Flower Child' making it a 13 track set. The song about Lenny's daughter Zoe was originally titled 'Zoe's Lullaby' and he wrote it a year earlier, in 1988, as a lullaby for her;

the song tells a story of a little girl's home of paradise, filled with flowers, angels, rainbows, gardens, oceans, jungle gym playgrounds and other treasures that little children love to have over a moving guitar part, with an orchestral piece coming in towards the end of the track making it a dreamer piece, which fits perfectly to the narrative of a lullaby with both music and lyrics in sync with each other. It also shows Lenny as a true songwriter for the future; a personal statement by a father showing, and sharing, his love for his daughter.

Let Love Rule, despite being a brilliant solo album, only achieved reasonable success in the USA and even after five years it still didn't make the 1 million mark, but sales outside the USA were considerably stronger. It sold over 2 million in Europe and was particularly strong in France, leading to a love affair with the country that remains to this day. However, Lenny would find much more commercial success in the coming decade, starting with *Mama Said*, his next album, in 1991. *Let Love Rule* would naturally of course have a resurgence, when Lenny released more commercially successful albums and the music buying public searched out his past releases, but for now sales on his debut in the USA were disappointedly modest. Because this was balanced with a much more favourable reaction elsewhere in the world, where his musical blend was far better initially received, the global picture wasn't in any way unsuccessful commercially. *Let Love Rule*, as expected, showcased all of Lenny's past musical influences, the album featuring soul, funk, rock and folk but mixed in a unique, intelligent and accomplished way.

In the middle of 1989 this discovery was musically refreshing in comparison to what the mainstream charts were offering. The music around at the time was extremely processed in sound - music sounded almost unnatural on record - and this never appealed to Lenny. Lenny's love affair with analogue and the vintage sound he loved had started, and from here onwards he never looked back. This sound and the way he openly embraced his influences were in the years ahead noted and sometimes criticised but ultimately the way that Lenny pursued the sound he wanted, and his openness and transparency in honouring his early influences, made him, in some way, unique.

What also makes a new discovery more exciting and exhilarating is for it to be musically from a single person, an individual, one person who has the rare accolade of playing most instruments on an album and being the sole writer of the songs. This put the musical descriptive resemblances from music journalists and album reviewers on to Bowie, Stevie Wonder and Prince, although this was very early and these comparisons were muted with caution and more described as 'influences' than comparisons. The production on *Let Love Rule* is a huge highlight, the sound is pure and organic and stays true to the traditional sounds that influenced Lenny previously. His opinions at the time were that the best albums, sound wise, came through in the 60s and 70s, and it was this feeling in the production he wanted to create, and in this respect he succeeded perfectly. It's this that stands out amongst the over-layered production often heard in the late 80s. Every instrument on the tracks can be heard perfectly and holds its own sound on the record. The Hammond organ is a particular highlight, fusing the sound together and giving a knowing nostalgic nod towards past influences. This is one of the reasons albums like *Let Love Rule* sound so fresh 20 years on, the production holding that primitive sound perfectly, a trait all the best albums retain so well that keeps them relevant many years into the future.

Following on from the inspiring surroundings in New York the album holds the hippie feel throughout, the title track advertising this direction for the 'Love is all you need' type mantra that's common in free thinking musicians. It's been done before of course, but it's pure and authentic in its thinking, a state of positive belief; in this instance 'Love is all you need' or 'All you need is Love' becomes 'Let Love Rule'. Even though the groove and the production remain solid Lenny allows for a horn solo to take hold, played by Karl Denson, and this takes over the track and becomes the focus, rising and stretching the sound. 'Let Love Rule' became Lenny's signature saying and he believed the sentence entirely; even to this day it's a statement he repeated at every concert, believing that if we let love rule it will conquer any conflict. Later, in 2012, his daughter Zoe persuaded Lenny to develop a new line of shoes for Toms, and amongst his designs were footwear printed with lyrics from this song.

Lyrically this theme throughout the album continues, although some of it feels a little unimaginative, 'sticking needles is veins' as an example; however, Lenny more than makes up for any of this with the raw and full-on emotional performance of his vocals. Songs like 'I Built This Garden for Us' also follow in this escapism, a hedonistic outlook where Lenny is starting with his own back yard, or in this case 'garden', to lead to a better and more inclusive world. The album, although headlined as a one-man band, obviously had musicians performing and assisting on it; these were Adam Widoff on guitars, the aforementioned Henry Hirsch on piano and organ, Karlly Gould on bass and Chad Smith on drums.

Adam Widoff was the first guitarist to play in Lenny's band and has credits for two early songs, 'Fear' on *Let Love Rule* and 'What Goes Around Comes Around' which was scheduled for Lenny's next album *Mama Said*. He was later replaced by Craig Ross who would go on to remain alongside Lenny from *Mama Said* onwards. Adam Widoff would go on to collaborate with many other artists in his own right including Stéphanie McKay, Stoney Clove Lane and Memorial Garage. The rest of the album featured Lenny on vocals, guitars, keyboards, bass, drums and percussion.

As 1989 came to a close Lenny appeared on the *Letterman* show and performed an acoustic version of 'Let Love Rule'. The performance featured just Lenny singing at the microphone with his guitar before he was interviewed by Letterman. He confessed that he met his wife backstage at a concert and that previously he had seen her in a magazine and told a friend he was going to marry her someday. He also talked about his daughter Zoe, who was a year old at this time.

Lenny started his *Let Love Rule* tour at the start of 1990 at various locations around the USA, drumming up a following and promoting his debut album. Naturally with Lenny being an instrumentalist in the studio he had to put together a backing band and would subsequently teach them his songs for touring and performing. Karl Denson took over saxophone, enabling him to replicate live the stunning solo on 'Let Love Rule', while his childhood friend 'Zoro' played drums. Adam Widoff played guitar with Lebron Scott on bass. Lenny watched Lebron Scott perform previously at a club in New York for Curtis Mayfield and recruited him for himself. Kenneth Crouch backed up the guitars with keyboards and the new band was complete, ready to rehearse, and set off on tour.

It started on February 1st 1990 and continued throughout the year. A month into the tour on March 16th 1990 it reached North America where Lenny played at First Avenue in Minneapolis, the venue made famous by his musical mentor Prince in his autographical movie *Purple Rain*. First Avenue is a venue very much connected to Prince and all his past successes; it was the location he played at whenever he was in town to try out new songs and new band members before going on tour, and it was around this time that Lenny first met his musical idol. Prince had heard *Let Love Rule* and invited Lenny to a studio he was working in, and they became friends. Lenny was flattered that Prince had recognised his music; he recalled Prince being extremely nice to him and found him very easy to get along with, and the two would hang out together over the years and meet up if they were in the same country on tour. Prince often invited Lenny on stage to jam with him at his many after-show and small club gigs at blues and jazz bars he was inclined to perform at after the main concert was finished. Prince also invited Lenny many times to his recording studio in Minneapolis, Paisley Park, and they would create music and jam together. Lenny recalled that they made and completed full songs together and Prince would simply give them to Lenny as a gift, never to be released. He would just simply call them 'Mementoes'.

Lenny and his band continued through North America and Canada before heading for Europe where sales for *Let Love Rule* were significantly higher than in the USA. Lenny played Germany, France and Holland before heading back to the US. Lenny also had his first taster in performing on a large scale as he was booked in to support some large established acts of the day. He was billed alongside Tom Petty and the Heartbreakers at Henry W. Kiel Municipal Auditorium in St Louis, followed by 2 shows at the Kemper arena in Kansas and another at Inglewood California. He played a one off show under his own billing in London at The Font in Kentish Town in May, followed by 3 shows in support of David Bowie at The Dodger Stadium Los Angeles, great exposure for the up and coming star.

Lenny next played a couple of festivals. He was booked in for a set at Roskilde, this year to be held from June 28th through to July 1st 1990, and was billed third during the day's events. The Roskilde Festival is a huge Danish music festival held annually south of Roskilde. It is one of the largest music festivals in Europe and the largest in Northern Europe. It first started in 1971 and the festival in 1990 was attended by around 130,000 visitors, so it was great exposure for any up and coming act. Lenny also appeared on mainstream TV and guested on *The Arsenio Hall Show* where he performed 'Let Love Rule' and was interviewed by Arsenio. He talked about his influences and Arsenio even took off Lenny's coat to wear, such was his fascination with his dress sense. Lenny spoke about the comparisons he was being given to John Lennon's solo work but also said he had not heard any Lennon material until his then manager gave him a tape. He also spoke about his wife and how proud he was to be married to her.

Lenny went down very well at all the performances he played at in support of his debut; however, there was another piece of success that was about to come Lenny's way when he had a studio session with a young poet and singer who was working with Prince. On a day off from filming and recording with the superstar she met Lenny and worked with him in the studio, and the results would be a huge.

During the touring Lenny continued writing and producing and spent time in studios around the USA working on various ideas for songs, and one of these in particular would be hugely successful. It was one of these ideas that produced a song that would give a worldwide hit for arguably the most famous female pop star on the planet, and it certainly gave Lenny kudos in the field of writing and producing for others. In October 1990 Madonna released 'Justify my Love' as a single from her new album *The Immaculate Collection*, her first hits package; it became a huge worldwide hit. It's ironic that Lenny had 'borrowed' a poet and singer working with Prince, one of the biggest and most successful *male* artists of all time, and it was created and recorded by Madonna, one of the biggest and most successful *female* artists of all time. He was certainly mixing within the right circles for success.

The song was written by Lenny alongside Ingrid Chavez with additional lyrics later added by Madonna. Ingrid Chavez was born in Albuquerque, New Mexico, but moved to Minneapolis in 1986 in search of stardom, which is not an obvious place to go to unless you're searching out one particular individual. She eventually met Prince and started to give him some of the poems that she was writing. Eventually Prince agreed to write and record an album around her poetry and put some music to them. He was also writing a movie that had gone through several cast changes and eventually he also cast her as the lead role in *Graffiti Bridge*, which he was also writing the soundtrack and music for. She eventually starred alongside Prince in the movie and featured on the subsequent soundtrack. It was during a day off from filming the movie that she went into the studio with Lenny and 'Justify my Love' was created, alongside another producer, André Betts. Andre would also work with Madonna on her next album, *Erotica*. Lenny and Andre composed the music while Chavez penned some lyrics over it that were based on a poem that she had previously written. She read them aloud and Lenny added the hook. On hearing the demo Madonna corrected a line or two and the song was completed, leading to a massive hit single. There was also of course the 'popular' music video, which was not without its own controversy, a shocker at the time in the early 90s, and being banned of course helped promote the single even more and gain notoriety. The single became a number one record in many countries around the world including the USA; however, the video itself was banned by MTV, which was a big deal in 1990, and many other outlets did the same. This made the video only available in record stores and as a result it immediately sold over 500,000 copies. Whether this was premeditated or not is debatable - sex and scandal always sell records - however, whichever way you look at it this single that Lenny produced and co-wrote was a massive worldwide hit. All was not harmonious however with the song itself, and would have been a shock and possible learning curve to

26

the young Lenny Kravitz, as this loose one-day jam session and demo turned itself into a law suit against him.

Ingrid Chavez was not credited for the song and sued Lenny. Later, in 1992, she eventually received an out-of-court settlement gaining a co-writing credit for the song. (Madonna's additional writing on the song was not questioned in the lawsuit). The song showed a different aspect in Lenny's writing; it's a song that encompasses different elements in his production, and it's certainly completely different to anything Lenny had written to this point and shows his versatility in the studio for experimenting in beats and sounds. The beat itself is based on a Public Enemy instrumental with the ending on the hook encompassing James Brown's 'Funky Drummer'. What's also a point of difference is the spoken word vocals Madonna is using, a departure from her previous style; interestingly this set her up and formed the direction of her next effort *Erotica*, again with Andre Betts, in which she spoke for most of the lyrics on the album as opposed to singing them. She also used the adult nature of the track as a prelude to *Erotica*, so the track is significant to the direction Madonna went in going forward around this time. *Erotica* was a concept album for Madonna, the concept being 'sex and romance', and was her first album under her new multimedia company Maverick, and also incorporated a book of explicit photos of the singer.

It's also clear listening to Ingrid Chavez that the spoken style is very much in keeping with the work she was doing with Prince around this period. She provides the spoken intro to Prince's 'Eye No', the first song on his 1988 album *Lovesexy*, and the songs she was currently working on with him all featured this soft-spoken delivery, which appeared on 'Justify My Love'. Ingrid Chavez released her debut album, co-written by Prince, a year later in 1991.

As the New Year rolled in Lenny started to move fast into writing what would be his second album, *Mama Said*. It was also around this time he started his long-term association with guitarist Craig Ross.

Craig Ross, born in Los Angeles, joined Lenny as he prepared to launch the *Mama Said* tour. They initially met in a billiard/pool room and they both felt instantly musically connected, and the connection remains to this day. This understanding added an instant ingredient to the songs Lenny would go on to create; Craig is one of the musicians who has arguably contributed the most musically to the songs of Lenny Kravitz over the years. Craig would also go on to have many spotlights and solos during concerts, some lasting over 8 minutes in length, and Lenny himself described him as 'the master' or 'the maestro'. In addition to his work with Lenny, Craig Ross has also collaborated with others and created his own band, The Broken Homes. He has also had connections with INXS, Stevie Ray Vaughan and Jerry Lee Lewis. The Broken Homes made three albums for MCA records and was produced by Led Zeppelin's Andy Johns. Other names have also been connected to Craig Ross including Sheryl Crow, Mick Jagger, BB King, Eric Clapton, Vanessa Paradis, Summer Cree, Nikka Costa and many others, but it would be his association writing, recording and touring with Lenny Kravitz from here onwards that would be most prominent in his career.

Things in Lenny's personal life had now taken a turn, and he had separated from his wife Lisa. This affected his writing during this period and these songs inevitably made their way to his album. This is a trait many great songwriters share, the ability to take the emotional baggage they are experiencing, whether that be heartache, grief, loss or any other personal emotion, and turn it to a song. These emotions channelled with a talent to write and record songs have made some of the greatest songs ever written; without these emotions of conflict or despair they simply would not, or could not, have been created. Lenny now had these emotions and songs were being crafted around the breakup of his marriage.

Again, on working through and forming what would eventually become the album *Mama Said* Lenny worked with Henry Hirsch as well as many other collaborators. On the first track scheduled for the album Lenny used a cover from the band The New York Rock Ensemble which was featured on their 1971 album *Roll Over*. The song 'Fields of Joy' also featured the late Michael Kamen who had an enviable CV to date within music. Michael was a highly sought-after arranger with successes with some of the biggest and most respected acts of the past 20 years;

28

these included Pink Floyd and Queen, for whom he composed the orchestration for 'Who Wants to Live Forever'. He worked with Eric Clapton, Aerosmith again for orchestration, Kate Bush on her album *The Red Shoes* and Bryan Adams. He had collaborated with The Eurythmics, Bryan Ferry and Metallica on *Nothing Else Matters*. He worked also within the realms of film and television conducting soundtracks and scores for some of the biggest and most successful movies on the big screen. His prestigious career earned him a nomination for two Academy Awards, and he won two Golden Globes, three Grammy Awards, two Ivor Novella Awards and an Emmy. It's an obvious understatement to say Michael Kamen was someone you wanted to have alongside you in the studio. He co-wrote the cover of 'Fields of Joy' with Lenny alongside Hal Fredricks and naturally the song became the first track on Lenny's new album. There was a reprise of the track on the album and they also contributed to this. The reprise was arranged by Lenny.

For the second track chosen for the album, 'Always on the Run', Lenny drafted in old schoolfriend Saul Hudson. Saul was now renamed Slash and had built a solid reputation of his own: at this time he was widely considered one of the world's great rock guitarists and was in Guns N Roses. Guns had signed with Geffen Records a few years earlier in 1986 and had massive success with *Appetite for Destruction* a year later in 1987. The following year they achieved a crossover number one record with 'Sweet Child o' Mine' featuring the now infamous guitar riff by Slash. Slash flew to the USA and worked with Lenny adding guitar to 'Always on the Run'. Slash had originally written this for Guns N Roses, but since Steven Adler couldn't do the drumming he took the track in basic form to Lenny and they reworked the song. It was also featured in the 1998 film *The Waterboy*. On 'Stand By My Woman' Lenny worked with former Spin Doctors member Anthony Krizan and on 'All I Ever Wanted' he worked with Sean Lennon, who was only 15 years of age. Sean played piano on the track. The three singles scheduled for the album were 'Always on the Run' followed by 'It Ain't Over 'Till It's Over' and then the aforementioned 'Fields of Joy'.

Continuing his growing live offering, Lenny kicked off his new tour in support of his forthcoming album. Following on from his first tour for *Let Love Rule*, Lenny now launched into the 'There is Only One Truth Tour', now encompassing material from his new album soon to be released. Lenny had recently been nominated for the Pollstar Concert Industry Awards Club Tour of the Year award for the 'Let Love Rule Tour' and his reputation as a live act was growing well. The new tour would naturally start to encompass larger stadiums as the anticipation for the new record started to gain momentum. On the release of the new album Lenny flew to Europe playing in England, Germany, Switzerland and France, before heading to Japan.

Mama Said was released on April 2nd 1991 and was an instant progression in all ways from its predecessor. It again landed many comparisons to Lenny's former influences, notably Prince, Hendrix, Curtis Mayfield and John Lennon. What's different on *Mama Said*, however, is Lenny is now identifying himself as an individual artist as opposed to being seen as an imitation of influences and styles. He was now seen as Lenny Kravitz, an artist who naturally blends and infuses his influences to create his own unique offering: it was a fusion, a modus operandi of past blends. It's a record that flows perfectly and again it has the production of its predecessor that makes it feel like it was recorded sometime in the 1970s, a classic feel in every way through the production, although the production is cleaner than on *Let Love Rule* and the sound becomes a little more polished. Every critic and every listener will choose their own highlights from an album but the overall stand-out tracks from the collection were 'Always on the Run' 'Fields of Joy 'and 'It Ain't Over 'Till It's Over'. This is one reason why they were selected as singles, as they sit as the strongest tracks on the album itself and are radio friendly. 'Always on the Run' as a first single is a quality statement from Lenny and forms a riff that countless cover bands will try and get their musical chops around for generations to come. Once mastered it's a classic that would stand the test of time for years if not decades ahead. It's a track that hits radio straight in the face and forms a great advert to the coming album, being released a month before the album itself on March 8th 1991.

'Always on the Run' also featured a great showcase music video showing Lenny at his live best, advertising beautifully the live performance that lay ahead in the promoting of the record. The video was directed by Jesse Dylan and features a very simple rock element of the song, in constant play, featuring Lenny and Slash and filmed in black and white. The track listing for the single also featured 'Butterfly' which also appeared on the album, 'Light Skin Girl from London', which also later featured on the 20th anniversary edition of *Let Love Rule*, and 'Always on the Run' as an instrumental. The contrast of these three tracks showcases wonderfully Lenny's versatility, a refreshing trait not many modern artists have and often overlooked in modern music. Artists are often pigeonholed into staying within a genre, or more to the point they stay within that genre because that's their level and they cannot, or don't have the ability, to move into other areas. *Mama Said* as an album was Lenny's commercial breakthrough. Although he had success with his Madonna hit single, because of the level of fame Madonna conveyed and also the notoriety of the music video, Lenny's involvement was overlooked, particularly from a commercial viewpoint. *Mama Said* addressed this and put Lenny on the map in his own right. It was often described as Lenny's 'Divorce Album' and it's clear to see why on the lyrical side of things: it's full of emotions comprising of loss, heartache and denial. Family matters are extended and Lenny sings of his daughter on 'Flowers for Zoe' as well as touching on protest themes with 'When the Morning Turns to Night'. Jazz sits well with Lenny and on 'What Goes Around Comes Around' he blends this with his Curtis Mayfield style vocals. It builds well, encompassing guitars, saxophone, horns and strings, and the results make it a very cool and outstanding track.

While on tour the second single was released from the album, on June 6th 1991. 'It Ain't Over 'Till It's Over' became a radio friendly smash and enjoyed significant airplay as Lenny toured. It's a repetitive tune, clearly in keeping with his personal situation at the time, but it turned into a hugely successful release reaching number 2 in the USA and number 11 in the UK, as well as various top 20 spots around the world. The track came with two additional songs, 'I'll Be Around' and 'The Difference is Why',

31

the latter an album track itself from *Mama Said*. 'It Ain't Over 'Till It's Over' became a signature tune for Lenny and a concert favourite for his growing fan base. The song was heavily inspired by the Motown sound and by Earth, Wind & Fire. The horn section at the end is actually played by the brass section of Earth, Wind & Fire. Lenny continued touring, with fans now picking up on the further chart success, and he played at Brixton Academy in London and then through Germany where he played in Hamburg and Berlin. When he reached the Netherlands, he played The Pinkpop Festival which averages around 60,000 fans per year; it was then Switzerland, France and Belgium before he headed to Japan where he played two dates on 6th and 7th July 1991. Also in July the third single from *Mama Said*, the cover version of 'Fields of Joy', was released. Clearly with the album having been on release since April and with this being the third single it didn't do well as a single in its own right, but it did serve as another recognisable track for Lenny to add to 'concert favourites' when performing live.

Through October 1991 Lenny and his band continued through North America and Canada before heading back to England. This time Lenny played the much larger Wembley Arena on November 24th with his following now significantly increasing. He again toured Europe on this wave with Germany, Italy, France and the Netherlands before returning to Canada with a New Year's Eve concert at Maple Leaf Gardens in Toronto. Lenny continued through the USA in February 1992 before he returned to the studio to work on what would be his next album.

As 1992 rolled in Lenny was now seen as an established worldwide star. With just two albums under his belt he had gathered enough material to maintain a live concert and keep the fans coming back for more. His interviews were also becoming noticed and the music world had someone new and exciting to take notice of. Naturally he was a long way from the huge established acts of the day, but his star was rising and his popularity was on the increase on the world stage. If he could now produce another quality album and keep this momentum going his fan base would only keep growing, and his popularity and status as a worldwide star could only get better. For Lenny it was time to ask, *Are You Gonna Go My Way...*

Photo © Benédicte Thibaudat

Bonjour, Going My Way?

The start of 1992 saw Lenny continuing touring through the USA in January and February before heading to Europe for a concert in Switzerland on May 7th. After this he returned to New York and started to put together songs that would appear on his next album *Are You Gonna Go My Way*. He started to work with other artists and carry on with the song writing in the studio, putting his ideas to tape. He was now estranged from his wife Lisa but despite this he always remained extremely close to his daughter Zoe, who was four years old at this time. He started spending time with French singer and actress Vanessa Paradis and started to write and record songs that would culminate in an album written and recorded solely for her.

Vanessa had found fame as a child singer with her song 'Joe Le Taxi' in 1987 when she was just fourteen years old, taken from her debut album *M&J*, standing for Marilyn and John. It became a number one single in France for nearly three months and a huge hit in the UK, even though it was sung in French. After she left school, she pursued her singing and acting career and in 1990 released her second album *Variations Sur Le Même T'aime* which featured the Lou Reed song 'Walk on the Wild Side', which again gave her a hit single. She also appeared in the movie *Noce Blanche* before going on to be the face of Coco Chanel in 1991 working with Jean Paul Goude. Here in 1992 she moved to the USA to start work with Lenny and put together ideas and songs for an album which would be her third. Despite the singles being successful from her first two albums the actual albums themselves performed poorly, and especially outside of her native France; working with Lenny would hopefully address this. She described being in the world of music, acting and modelling at such a young age as a feeling of lost identity. She described feeling like she forgot who she really was, so moving to New York and spending six months there away from this world and working with Lenny had allowed her to find herself and to be her own person. Lenny had his full band in the studio and Vanessa started to follow Lenny's vocals and guides to the songs he had written. In hindsight listening to this record it does sound very much like a Lenny Kravitz album but with the vocals removed and Vanessa Paradis singing her own. It's a technique very much in keeping with the way Prince often recorded other singers when writing and recording with them. The album would become the most successful for Vanessa and remains so to this date.

The album was released on September 21st 1992 and yielded two singles, 'Be My Baby' and 'Sunday Mornings'. Initially there was an extra track recorded entitled 'Gotta Have It' but this was later omitted and remained only on the Japanese version of the album. The album was created again at Waterfront Studios in New Jersey and was attributed to Lenny as producer but Vanessa took creative control over the album, much more so than in her previous releases. Again, Lenny uses his production techniques in full glory giving the album a unique feel compared to the standard sounds created in 1992. It's very much in keeping with the *Let Love Rule* feeling, using techniques to make the album feel you're listening to something 'vintage' and timeless. The creation of the album was filmed for a one-hour special released later in 1993, eventually March, and featured studio footage of Lenny and the band working with Vanessa in various stages of production. 'Be My Baby' became a hit single and did very well, reaching number 6 in the UK and number 5 in France. The album itself reached platinum status in France and eventually reached around a million copies worldwide.

The busy period of writing with others continued for Lenny when he worked with Mick Jagger as he composed another solo album. Mick was working on his third solo album away from The Rolling Stones entitled *Wandering Spirit*, which was set to be released in February 1993. Lenny sang with Jagger on the track 'Use Me' which was previously a hit for Bill Withers in 1972. The album was a great success for Mick Jagger and was critically acclaimed; it's an album that showcases all of Jagger's skills as a songwriter and his ability to tone down the Rolling Stone typical rock 'n' roll sound for a new and inclusive one, encompassing synthesisers. The record was co-produced by Rick Rubin and this kept the production of the album clean and uncomplicated. Lenny's own vocals on 'Use Me' fitted in perfectly with the track and added to his musical associations and ability to work in a variety of styles and genres. The album was released in February 1993 and became a worldwide hit for Mick, a month before Lenny planned the release of his own third album.

Staying at Waterfront Studios Lenny completed his third album *Are You Gonna Go My Way*, again with Henry Hirsch, during the latter months of 1992. The first single was the title track itself, released on February 22nd 1993, which scored Lenny his first worldwide mainstream hit. Because the song was only actually released as an 'airplay single' it was not eligible to chart on the Billboard Hot 100, the main chart in the US, but it immediately rose to the top and reached number one in the US Mainstream Rock chart, and also had huge success in the UK and reached number four in the charts. It had a massive amount of airplay both in the UK and the US and around the rest of the world. The album followed the following month, released on 9th March, and on the back of the lead single riding high in the charts, and the previous touring, the release of the new record immediately pushed Lenny further forward into superstar status. As a single itself the lead single became a classic for Lenny, becoming an almost signature tune for him going forward; it also become a huge rock anthem in the 1990s and beyond. Further to the success of the single there was a crossover into other media which pushed the song even further. Video gaming was becoming huge business and key games at the time, Gran Turismo, Guitar Hero World Tour and Guitar Hero Live, all featured the song, gaining further popularity. This allowed it to reach those who would ordinarily not have heard the single or indeed heard of Lenny Kravitz. The tune became huge all over the gaming world as well as through airplay on radio and television.

The album has a cover indicative of rock stardom and it's clear that Lenny was now trying to move himself into the big league. It shows him in a provocative pose and looking rebellious. He is slightly blurred and being photographed, the unknown female photographer offset slightly with her back turned; the shot has a retro feel with the clothing to match, setting the tone for the record. The feeling of the album again goes straight to the heart of Lenny's influences and 'remains past'; it's clear again that Lenny is following bygone vintage trends to intertwine into his sound. Although this was an ongoing theme for Lenny and often cited by critics it's clear that whatever they may have felt about Lenny's influence of past sounds his songwriting craft and production still pushes him to the forefront. The album is another step forward and again is more accomplished than his previous albums, and of course the similarities remained with Lennon, Curtis Mayfield, Prince and Hendrix. That said, it's not a bad mix to be associated with, even though the association was often described as imitation rather than a present individual sound. It's an album that is extremely enjoyable; it's consistent and the classic rock reproduced shows again all the influences being brought together. Of course this holds the risk of being unoriginal, but Lenny's strengths in his production, delivery and craft eliminate this. Add this to his growing back catalogue and it only gave him added kudos as a rock star. The album helped elevate Lenny further up the scale, and the video for the album title track was heavily featured on MTV, capturing Lenny and his band perfectly, again showcasing a live spectacle and providing a great advert for him for his live performances and future tours. It featured Lenny and the band surrounded by people dancing with lots of slow motion closeups of Lenny in various 'guitar shred' poses. It was directed by Mark Romanek.

'Believe' was released on May 10th 1993 and is in rock ballad territory. The track has string orchestration throughout and again was co-written with Henry Hirsch, who also contributed to the orchestration in the track. Lenny explores the themes of freedom and eternal grace in the song and faith in God. The accompanying music video for 'Believe' was directed by French Director Michel Gondry and is based on Stanley Kubrick's *Space*

Odyssey from 1968. The single came with two versions, the standard track and an acoustic. The other tracks on the maxi disc were an acoustic version of 'Sister' and a track called 'For the First Time'. The vinyl record only contained the two versions of 'Believe'. As a single in its own right it reached number 60 on the US Billboard chart and 30 in the UK, performing in similar positions around the world.

The release of *Are You Gonna Go My Way* gave Lenny for the first time a record in his own right; he was fairly well known before but was far from a household name. On his debut album most of the interviews and press that surrounded the record were regarding his marriage to Lisa Bonet and of course his mother, who was herself famous. This gave Lenny a sort of showbiz 'in' and pulled the focus away from him as an individual. He wasn't so much Lenny Kravitz the rock star multi-instrumentalist but the husband and son of a famous actresses. He was also often seen as an imitator of past sounds, using techniques to replicate them, and songs written in the style of others, more of a novelty than anything unique and inspirational. *Mama Said* was harshly described as his divorce album, and musically and more importantly lyrically it references his relationship often, which again drew press attention to the relationship, and again this focused on his showbiz connections. It did however give Lenny his first major hit single with 'It Ain't Over 'Till It's Over', but again this is drawing on his past relationship. The title track itself, 'Are You Gonna Go My Way', is typical of a great songwriter and how they craft and form certain songs that go on to be huge hits around the world: Lenny and Craig Ross were just jamming in the studio with no particular thing in mind and the whole thing happened within five minutes. As they were jamming Lenny felt that there was something happening and that they were on to something; he told Henry to turn the tape machines on and they played it. He then wrote the lyrics on a brown paper bag. Lenny was still living in the loft on Broome Street at the time, and he went back to the studio and sang it the next day, and that was it. Lenny said the song is about Jesus Christ, whom he referred to as the Ultimate Rock Star. It's about how God gives choice to man about where to turn.

Moving forward from all this, it set things up for *Are You Gonna Go My Way* to be Lenny's first album in his own right, unshackling himself from the past connections. The songwriting on the album isn't as obviously autobiographical as his previous albums, although naturally there are songs written that represent where Lenny was at the time in relationships and life in general, a trait all great songwriters possess. Even the Bahamian Island of 'Eleuthera' has its own song, referencing his mother's background and where Lenny would eventually set up a home. The album became his first top 20 hit, and in 1993 this was something still relevant before the chart system in the years ahead imploded on itself and became irrelevant on any given chart positioning. It went double platinum and in keeping with his past two records became a huge hit outside the US, topping the charts in the UK and Australia. It's interesting to note also that Lenny was instantly bigger around the world than in the US, where perhaps the record buying and concert going public only saw Lenny Kravitz as Lenny Kravitz and were unaware of any connections to anyone else. Furthermore, in the USA Lenny only released 'Believe' and 'Heaven Help' from the album. The latter is not even written by Lenny himself but by Terry Britten, who had previously worked with Tina Turner, and again throughout the album he is assisted heavily on guitars by Craig Ross. The title track was only actually released as an 'airplay only single' which put focus more on the album as a whole. On 'Believe' Lenny explored themes that have stayed with him throughout his career: he sings about the power within faith and explores the following of God, self and positive thinking, which all equates to love, and his 'Let Love Rule' outlook. Michel Gondry, who would go on to direct a string of surreal videos for Björk, The White Stripes, and others, directed the outer space-themed music video with Lenny shown as an astronaut.

What's important to note so far in the career of Lenny Kravitz is in connection to that what we are seeing around him at the time, his identity is breaking through, and this identity would remain with him for the next 25 years and beyond. At this time, in 1993, hip hop was the up and coming genre in music and it would continue to be so. Rock and roll was starting to become a little tired and tested. The very notion of creating music with guitars, bass, piano and drums, and the songwriting raw skill and talent involved, was being quietly smeared at as easy beats that were programable at the touch of a button were becoming the mainstream. Furthermore, the creators of these tunes held themselves in high esteem, as if this they had an equal talent to someone like Lenny Kravitz, which of course musically they didn't - they were a world away. What is significant however is that this movement was initially just through music but now, over the past few years, a major shift had happened. It moved into fashion and culture and this kept the momentum strong in all aspects of general life. Many mainstream musicians started to take note and brought the hip hop rap element into their sound, to make it blacker, to be seen to be moving with the times. Lenny however, to his credit, stuck to his guns and simply belted out his mix of vintage sounding rock influenced by the great sounding records of the 60s and 70s, and in this environment which would grow stronger his style and sound would become further away from the mainstream and, importantly, what radio stations were looking for on their playlists, in order to be on trend and up to date. Even to this day, although Lenny has a huge list of brilliant radio friendly tunes it is still the same handful of songs that are continually played.

Lenny started the promotion of the record with a performance on *Saturday Night Live* in April 1993, a month after release. The show had actress Kirstie Alley as the special guest, and Lenny performed 'Are you Gonna Go My Way' and 'Always on The Run', two huge songs in every sense of the word and even more so combined back to back. After this he travelled back to Europe and again performed at The Pinkpop Festival in the Netherlands; he then performed through Germany in June. The love affair with Europe continued as he held concerts in Switzerland, Italy, France and Spain before landing in England to perform at Glastonbury on June 26th. The Glastonbury appearance was a last minute one as The Red Hot Chili Peppers, who were due to headline, pulled out at the last minute due to Flea suffering from Chronic Fatigue Syndrome. Lenny was drafted in and played his set; the write ups of Lenny's performance however were not favourable mainly due to the fact that the crowd were obviously there to see someone else. In truth it didn't matter who was the replacement - it would never have been a substitute for what the fans were there for, which was The Red Hot Chili Peppers and not Lenny Kravitz. Lenny travelled back to Europe shortly after and during July played France, Germany, Switzerland, Sweden and Norway before then heading back home to start the US leg of the tour.

After a performance in Dallas on September 2nd 1993 Lenny performed at the MTV Music Video Awards where he won the award for Best Male Video. He performed a brilliant performance of 'Are You Gonna Go My Way' at the awards; it showcased Lenny in pure Rock God status commanding the microphone and shredding through the set; alongside him was Craig Ross looking equally the rock showman taking his turn for the guitar solo. Raised above in a Prince 'Sheila E' type visual was the future wife of Carlos Santana, drummer Cindy Blackman, who had just joined Lenny's touring band and had previously auditioned for him down the phone. There weren't a great deal of female rock drummers around at this time, even though gender has nothing to do with drumming, apart from the aforementioned Sheila E who toured with Prince in the late 1980s, so this gave a refreshing and more stimulating effect to the live performance. Her looks and drumming style completed a very cool and tight performing rock band. Cindy also had a background in jazz as well as rock so suited Lenny's many variations in his sound. This performance showcased Lenny as a true live musician and demonstrated to the masses, on the back of the lead single flying high in the charts and airplay around the globe, that he was someone to see. On September the 9th Lenny repeated the performance on *The David Letterman Show*, gaining more exposure for his tour, which continued through September and October in the US finishing in Seattle and Vancouver on October 31st. He then flew to Europe once again where his album was gaining attention and the title track was high again in the airplay charts.

Lenny's venues were now getting larger and he was filling arenas up to 15,000 capacity. He now had a back catalogue of material within his first three albums that could run a concert with all the thrills and spills for up to two hours and beyond. With his virtuoso he was able to drift from guitarist, frontman, singer and pianist throughout the show, keeping it tight and compelling with the variation in his songs. Typically, the show ran with the following set list around this time: 'Is There Any Love in Your Heart', 'Fields of Joy', 'Stop Draggin' Around', 'Freedom Train', 'Always on the Run', 'My Precious Love', 'Sister', 'Are You Gonna Go My Way', 'I Build This Garden for Us' and 'Mr. Cab Driver'. The concerts would always end with 'Let Love Rule' becoming a signature end of concert song with full audience participation and often with Lenny moving into the crowd; the show of course would vary from time to time but the core stayed the same. As the tour travelled again through Europe Lenny made an appearance on German TV on the ZDF Pop Show on November 20th 1993, where he performed 'Are You Gonna Go My Way' and 'Heaven Help' before two shows in France. With his popularity rising Lenny returned to England where previously he had played venues such as The Brixton Academy, which holds just under 5,000. Now, starting on November 27th 1993, he was able to play Wembley Arena with the show a sell out at the 12,500-seater stadium. He played again on the 28th November before playing The Scottish Exhibition Centre in Glasgow, The Sheffield Arena and The National Exhibition Centre in Birmingham. He then jetted off for seven concerts in Australia from 5th February 1994 through to the 16th before finishing this leg of the tour in Japan on February 23rd and 25th.

After the Japanese tour, and in light of Lenny's MTV Video award, he was invited to play a session for *MTV Unplugged*. At this time the series was at the height of its popularity and notoriety. Lenny recorded his session for the series at the Sony Music Studios in New York on March 14th. The band as before played brilliantly with Lenny at the front and Craig Ross to his left, Cindy Blackman sitting behind with her huge hair looking more like a star in her own right on the drums. The concert started with a bluesy version of 'Are You Gonna Go My Way' with Ross playing slide guitar. Lenny also played harmonica during the set, adding to the blues and acoustic feel. 'Believe' followed, then 'Rosemary', 'Just be a

Woman', 'Sister', 'Always on the Run' and 'My Precious Love'. The superb set concluded with the usual 'Let Love Rule'.

Shortly after the *MTV Unplugged* session another song gained a following which Lenny had recently penned. While not a single Lenny co-wrote a song with Aerosmith's musicians Steven Tyler and Joe Perry that featured on the band's eleventh studio album *Get a Grip*. The album became a huge hit for the 'Bad Boys from Boston' selling in excess of 20 million copies. The album produced many hit singles for the band and Lenny co-wrote the song 'Line Up' which featured on the album; in addition Lenny also provided backing vocals. What's surprising however was although the song was not drafted as a single it gained a huge amount of attention when it was given its own full length showing in the movie *Ace Ventura Pet Detective* starring Jim Carey, which was released that year in February. The track showcases Ace Ventura going through various scenes and brought a great deal of focus to the song. The movie itself was a huge box office hit grossing a reported $107 million and costing just $15 million to produce. Although the movie was released in February it remained on the big screen in theatres around the world all through the first half of 1994, gaining more attention to the track. It also added to Lenny's reputation as a songwriter and collaborator, now with a growing list of key musical figures he had worked with. This continued in July of this year when Teena Marie released her tenth studio album, *Passion Play*, including the song 'Main Squeeze' featuring Lenny. The album was the first since her departure from a major label and was released on her own independent label Sarai Records. As a result of the lack of backing from a large label it didn't perform as well as her previous records but was very well received by her hardcore fanbase.

Lenny continued with collaborations while mid tour in the USA when he worked with Stevie Wonder for a cover version of a song for a tribute album for one of his early influences. In July 1994 rock band Kiss were celebrating their 20th anniversary; their first self-titled album was released in 1974. This new tribute album featured a variety of musicians. It was renamed *Kiss my Ass; Classic Kiss Regrooved* and Lenny and Stevie's version of 'Deuce' was the opening track on the album. The album spent 13 weeks in the charts and was certified gold status. 'Deuce' itself is one of the band's most popular tracks and a concert opener when they toured. It became one of the singles from the album with Stevie Wonder also providing backing vocals and harmonica.

In September 1994 Lenny concluded the tour in support of *Are You Gonna Go My Way* in Chicago. It had been an incredible success for him. It was an album that gave Lenny a huge hit single and his popularity as a live act and songwriter was growing rapidly. He was of course still tagged with being a sort of songwriting chameleon, drawing from and replicating other influences past and present, but this did not detract from the fact that he was still a brilliant live act with the ability to create catchy pop and rock sounds in the true musical sense. This also gave Lenny a sort of identity of his own: you could easily see and hear his influences, and he was able to replicate them on record and didn't shy away from them. Hendrix, Lennon, Prince, Curtis Mayfield were all elements of his sound. Some critics clearly felt that he was replicating them too much - being so studious of his influences had made him unoriginal - but some simply didn't care, especially his huge legion of fans who flocked to see him all over the world; it was good music and that's all that mattered.

The three albums to this point Lenny had produced show a musician with a songwriting craft growing rapidly in the music industry. Lenny had taken all the individual elements of his past influences and unashamedly tried to recreate them, using vintage techniques to encapsulate the sound he wanted, a sound that felt right and nodded to the great albums he loved so much. His look, and that of his band, also had this vintage rock look and his image was again in keeping with this feeling. *Are You Gonna Go My Way* unshackled Lenny and with the major worldwide hit and his constant touring he had established himself on the world stage. It was an album that established Lenny in his own right and an album that put his past connections behind him. He concentrated on the music, the album, and the live performances, and it worked. He was now seen as Lenny Kravitz the rock star; he was a musician that other artists wanted to work with, a producer, a songwriter and an electric performer. And of course, with the hit that the album was, new fans discovered him and embraced his back catalogue,

44

hearing them for the first time with fresh ears, which only enhanced his status. In addition, he was a collaborator who was sought after heavily: it didn't matter how big a star you were, or how big your talent was, Lenny Kravitz was someone who would add value to what you were doing.

Are You Gonna Go My Way and the tour that followed the album had given Lenny in the past year prolonged success, but despite this, and all the achievements he had made, Lenny was feeling frustrated. The music industry was changing, and it was changing rapidly. Recording contracts used to be the holy grail, and Lenny himself searched for one, a long term one, one that supported his artistic growth as a musician. Now they were becoming challenged: two of the biggest male pop stars on the planet, George Michael and Prince, were engaged in very public legal battles with their own record labels, and there was a distinct lack of musicians coming through to modern day music. Artists like Lenny were starting to look obsolete within the changing face of the music industry as artists were using less instrumentation in favour of computerised technology. This of course meant that there was less 'skill' required for talented musicians. In short, musicians in the true sense of the word, as people who *played instruments* and created music were becoming less popular, and the modern-day recording contract was being challenged as artists fought for artistic freedom over commercial direction imposed by record companies.

In Lenny's opinion, straightforward rock and roll and the musicians that created it were becoming a thing of the past; it wasn't 'on trend' anymore. Of course, he had respect for other artists but this wasn't his thing; he was about the creative process in its pure sense and creating music with musicians using the studio to replicate the sound he wanted, a pure sound that wasn't processed. He was also looking around him, and felt that, quite correctly, that lesser talents were seemingly more popular. Lenny's early influences, which he held in such esteem, were, at this point in time, becoming a bit of a novelty and not taken seriously. These highly influential musicians' bands and singers, some of the greatest in the history of pop and rock music, were being overshadowed by new up and coming bands and performers that

45

frankly would not have had the ability to even stand with them on the same stage night after night. To someone like Lenny Kravitz who was schooled by such artists this had to have been comical to say the least. Musicians who spent time in jazz bars, clubs and bars honing their skills, learning their craft over years of playing, were to be respected, and rightly so. Now success was becoming instant, you didn't need this, and record companies didn't have the patience to wait for artists to get established, they wanted success immediately, and so the search was different, and these acts were spreading fast. The very industry was being challenged and questioned and major established artists were taking on the establishment and record contracts that they perceived to be old fashioned, controlling and stifling artistic freedom. It was looking like standard bands who created rock music were falling behind to a new threat both on recording and performing. There were also many artists and bands who were becoming successful who could easily lip-sync their way through, and this was seen as acceptable; behind the scenes there were also cultural movements dictating what was fashionable and what was cool particularly through hip-hop and the misogynistic music videos that this represented.

Whether Lenny had his tongue in his cheek or not when he wrote his next single, a reflection on rock and roll in the mid 90s, is debatable. Did the above factors bother him enough to write a scathing attack on the situation or was he simply mocking the talentless self-absorbed non-musicians invading the space? However it was viewed from a pure musician's perspective it did look at the time as if rock and roll was in trouble, it was fading, it was dying, or even worse... *Rock and Roll is Dead*.

Photo © Benédicte Thibaudat

The End of Rock & Roll

As a songwriter in every sense of the word, Lenny's frustrations had an honest approach, an approach that led its way into songs. Lenny was starting to get despondent with the music industry, and he was now writing songs that dealt with this, and the writing of material during this period, which would eventually make its way to his next album, to be titled *Circus*, was very difficult. He was also now dealing with a personal matter when his mother was diagnosed with breast cancer and was fighting the disease.

It's true that the music industry was changing rapidly at this point as we enter 1995. The internet was emerging fast and record sales in the true sense of the word were diminishing. A number one record on the Billboard Charts would be selling half the amount it would 10 years previously as different distribution was becoming more prominent and forward-thinking musicians were embracing this trend. This was mainly because it cut out the middle-man or record company: the future looked like it was moving to direct distribution as opposed to a long-term contract that tied an artist down. The chart system was becoming fragmented and illegal downloads were becoming common, there was also a distinct lack of meaningful acts emerging, and the mid 1990s was becoming an alien world for artists like Lenny Kravitz, artists with true musicality.

Lenny spent the first half of 1995 working on and putting together his fourth studio album, *Circus*, at Waterfront Studios, New Jersey, again recorded by Henry Hirsch. The album was also additionally worked on in France and at Compass Point Studios in The Bahamas. Again, he had his usual musicians working with him: Craig Ross played electric guitar throughout the album and

Henry Hirsch provided bass, electric piano and also mixing. Craig Ross also co-wrote 'Beyond the 7th Sky', 'In My Life Today' and 'The Resurrection'. The title track itself was credited to Gerry DeVeaux and Terry Britten who had a long and established producing and writing career himself working with Diana Ross, Tina Turner and Michael Jackson among many others.

The first single was released on July 26th leaving no doubt as to Lenny's opinions on the current music industry as it stood, although Lenny claimed that this was not the case and it was misrepresented. It apparently was more in line with Lenny calling out those within the industry, the fakers, the posers, the talentless pretenders getting away with it, as opposed to any direct protest. In short it was Lenny taking the piss out of others as he looked at the musical competition, the popular bands and artists that filled the charts and those that were currently popular; he was looking at the rock 'n' roll lifestyle that surrounded him. The very nature of the song however cannot be ignored and gives an insight into what Lenny thought of these individuals who lacked the musical talent to be in the same game. 'Rock and Roll Is Dead' as a protest of any sort was played down by Lenny: he claimed the track was misunderstood and you had to go deeper and not look at it at face value; he claimed he was not being serious and was just being a clown, having fun with the track; the fact however that the song follows in the same vein and overall feel of 'Are You Gonna Go My Way' led that deeper meaning to be missed, and probably explains why he had to defend the questioning of it. Interestingly, and in response, Prince released his own song 'Rock and Roll Is Alive (And It Lives In Minneapolis)' shortly after; it was a B-side to his single 'Gold' from the album *The Gold Experience*, which he was protesting widely to have released, because his record company Warner Bros were holding it back.

Despite the focus on the title itself the song only brushed the charts reaching number 75 in the US Billboard Hot 100, and reaching number 22 in the UK. The video is shot in black and white and shows Lenny shredding the guitar with lots of silhouettes of the band behind; there are also several sequences that show artistic backgrounds in keeping with the theme. The video was directed by Ruven Afanador and the storyboard for the theme of the video was by Andrew Trovaioli. It was a disappointing start, especially after the success of his previous album and the crossover into the mainstream. Lenny also had a growing reputation as a live act so his core fan base was growing rapidly, so the fact that the first single didn't carry on the momentum was surprising. On release the track listing contained 'Rock and Roll Is Dead', 'Another Life' and a live version of 'Are You Gonna Go My Way'; another version contained another track 'Is It Me, Is It You?' Lenny was nominated for a Grammy Award for Best Male Rock Vocal Performance for the song a year later in 1996; this would be Lenny's third nomination in the category.

For promotion of the album Lenny planned a tour which was scheduled to start in London in September, the same month that the album was released. The actual release date of *Circus* came on September 12th 1995, two months after the release of 'Rock and Roll Is Dead'. The album did well and became reviewed as just that, an album, as opposed to a collection of songs that would generate hit singles, especially when on reflection to his back catalogue; reviews however were yet again mixed. One thing that was certain was that his hardcore fan base flocked to it. Lenny with *Circus* had stayed within an area that was safe for him: he played to his strengths. Now at 31 years old he was established and his blend of soul and classic infused rock was where he was sitting, and sitting successfully. One thing that *Circus* didn't have however was any real commercial hit songs within it, which gives it a point of difference from previous albums he had released. This was seen by some as a disappointment as this momentum of having something that the album could focus on was missed - nothing was instantly catchy, which moved the focus onto the album as a 'whole piece' as opposed to there being anything that individually stood out on its own. This of course could have been intentional: it had been done before on many albums in the past, particularly concept albums that stay within a certain theme, and looking at the single listing from the album it doesn't look like any kind of grand effort to break the mainstream charts. The songs fit in with the concept of the album as a narrative but they lack catchy radio friendly hooks to warrant consistent airplay. This of course had nothing to do with Lenny - the overall riff on 'Rock and Roll is

Dead' is musically superior to 99% of anything charting on radio at this time in 1995, it just simply didn't fit, so maybe the tongue in cheek was in fact correct.

The album has Lenny sitting in a stable groove. It moves well between his established territory, that of an early 70s album that you have just discovered and something of early 70s soul. Again, there is the comparison to Prince with references and phrases but overall Lenny is happy sitting within his comfort zone on the album. Some cited *Circus* as the weakest of Lenny's albums to this point, with the reason being that he didn't change his style in any distinctive manner, but tried instead to replicate himself from the sound of 'Are You Gonna Go My Way'. In addition, 'Rock and Roll Is Dead' sounds like it could be a B-side throw away to 'Are You Gonna Go My Way', a similar tune but one that lacks the overall killer hook. The album as a whole piece however is different and shows Lenny again playing to where his talent and scope are fullest, in the series of ballads and lightly psychedelic mid-tempo pop numbers, which prove to be his real strength.

Lenny's fan base, as all fan bases should do, largely ignored the reviews of *Circus*; it was another album with more tracks in the style they loved and it added to Lenny's arsenal of touring material. *Circus* would not go on to be seen as a classic from the Lenny Kravitz discography but despite the fact that it didn't reach the sales from his previous albums it held one important factor linking back to his core fan base: it was his first album to crack the Top 10 on the Billboard chart. *Circus* went gold, selling well over 500 thousand copies. In fact, it eventually went gold in Argentina, France, Netherlands, Switzerland and the UK. It was even more successful outside the USA where even higher sales were achieved, in Japan for example it eventually went platinum. The Japanese version also had an additional track 'Another Life' and this was a key area of touring for Lenny, where his fan base was strong. What do critics know?

There comes a time in an artist's career when they exit the masses and create their own following, a personal fan base, a hard core. If this base is big enough it's the perfect scenario for any artist; they may of course not hit the dizzy high points of the chart system but the music is reaching the people that matter, and this is important. Lenny with *Circus* didn't hit the sales achieved from his previous albums but what he did do with the album was have it bought, and bought quickly, by the following he had amassed around the world. His own core fan base. The music industry was changing and changing quickly, the chart system was becoming ever more fragmented and the rise of direct distribution by forward thinking artists was shaking the traditional sales route. Around this time David Bowie, Peter Gabriel and Prince were all looking at multimedia packages to distribute their music direct to fans, direct from them to the consumer's own home, or more to the point to their own computers. Gabriel and Bowie were playing with the idea, but Prince was more serious and saw this as the very future of the industry; he was right, and his own pursuits around this time led the way as the chart system imploded from the traditional perspective. This grew separate charts, separate 'downloads' and pushed the traditional sales route of buying records and albums in various directions. In essence it didn't really matter from here onwards if your sales had dipped slightly as these dips were gained in other areas, such as touring and giving it direct to the fan base. The bottom line comes with talent: if you have it, and can play, people will always follow you and you'll fill out stadiums, and this in turn will create your own fan base, your own direct promotion - and Lenny had this when he toured.

On September 16th 1995 Lenny kicked of his tour in promotion of *Circus* in London at Shepherds Bush Empire. The 'Circus Tour' added more songs into the setlist as Lenny added in songs from *Circus* itself. He added 'Tunnel Vision', 'Circus' and 'Can't Get You Off My Mind' which made sense as they were the main singles from the record, but the set list changed slightly as the tour progressed. He next played Belgium and then an appearance on French TV at Canal+, Nulle Part Ailleurs in Paris where he played 'Rock and Roll is Dead' before a full concert at Cirque d'Hiver Bougilone on September 22nd.

Lenny released the second single from the album, the title track itself, on September 26th while on mid tour in Europe. The CD contained the album version, an acoustic version, 'Tunnel Vision' and 'Are You Gonna Go My Way'.

Lenny played a one-off concert in Madrid before moving to northern Europe where he played another TV show in the Netherlands at Grand Gala Du Disc 1995, performing 'Circus' on the show. He then played two shows at Paradiso Grote Zaal in Amsterdam on October 5th and 6th before moving to Germany. While in Amsterdam and before the concert on the 5th at Paradiso Lenny decided he would get his guitar painted. He went to a local gallery in the afternoon before the concert, Gallery Rosa Lisa, and asked Dutch artist Rosa Lisa Villa if she would come over to paint it. She rushed over with some paint before the concert and painted it while Lenny practised vocal exercises before going on stage. The concert itself was delayed by around 15 minutes because the paint wasn't dry and they kept it in front of a heater. There are photos of Lenny with his new guitar, freshly painted, from this concert, and it was rumoured afterwards in Germany that someone stole it, so there was a sad ending.

With the album doing particularly well in Japan Lenny and the band travelled across to play four dates from November 9th through to November 21st; however, news from back home prompted Lenny to return as soon as he could, which he did immediately after the last Japanese concert in Tokyo.

While Lenny was touring Japan, he had received a call from back home that his mother's condition had deteriorated and she was extremely ill. As soon as his schedule allowed, he returned quickly back to the US to be by her side. Lenny arranged to stay with record producer Rick Rubin who he had previously worked with alongside Mick Jagger on *Wandering Spirit*. Rick was working with Johnny Cash at the time on his album *American Recordings II: Unchained.* Lenny got off the plane and went straight to the hospital where his mother was alive but fading. Thinking that she may have just a few days left to live he went to the house to take a shower and get some food but on the way there his mother died, and on arriving at the house Lenny received the phone call. She had died on 2nd December 1995 of breast cancer at the age of 66, only a day after his daughter Zoë's birthday. As he put the phone down from the hospital Johnny Cash and his wife June were walking down the stairs and Johnny asked Lenny how he was; still fazed by the call Lenny told Johnny and June the news.

They consoled him there and then and were of great comfort in what must have been a devastating moment for Lenny. Lenny reflected on this moment in a single released in 2018: the song 'Johnny Cash' appears on the album *Raised Vibration* and is in tribute to this moment of humanity and kindness that Johnny Cash and his wife June Carter gave to him at a time of immense shock and personal grief.

Lenny played two shows shortly after his mother's passing at KROQ Almost Acoustic Christmas at Universal Amphitheatre in California on December 17th and 18th. He then took a break before moving into 1996 with the tour continuing at the end of January with two shows in Los Angles on January 26th and 27th. Also in January the second single from *Circus* was released, 'Can't Get You Off My Mind'. It's Lenny Kravitz at his melodic and songwriting best, bringing together perfectly many of his past influences through to the song. He said of the opening lyric, 'Life is just a lonely highway', that it felt at the time of writing like an almost Spinal Tap moment, a cliché of a line, a pastiche. The song went on to be a concert favourite, especially as an acoustic number, and is a stand out track in any Lenny Kravitz compilation. The *Circus* tour was again met with great reviews, with the new album giving more songs to the set list, Lenny adding 'The Resurrection' as an opening track as the tour moved through North America and Canada. This song was scheduled to be the third single from the album, and he performed on *The Late Show with David Letterman* on 15th February before he moved the tour to Europe starting in France on February 20th.

Again, as before Lenny's popularity in Europe exceeded that in the US at this time. He played his way through large stadiums in Sweden, four shows in Germany, Switzerland, Austria and The Czech Republic. Demand was so high that after a show in Milan on March 16th he returned to Germany for two additional shows on March 19th and 20th 1995. He returned to England and again sold out Wembley Arena on March 23rd, which proved again that even though *Circus* was played down by critics and journalists his fan base and the core that wanted to see him live was undeterred; his music was reaching the people that mattered and he was able to sell out stadiums all over Europe and the world. The concert reviews again were fantastic: Lenny's ability to mix the hard edged rock sound with psychedelic pop melodies and ballads was a live show winner, his music and the way his band performed it night after night was electric and brought him countless returning fans wherever he travelled. He returned to Spain after Wembley and played three shows before he played France again and finally the Netherlands, which concluded the European tour of *Circus* on April 8th 1996.

Back in the USA Lenny played at Kiss Concert 1996 on June 1st, as he travelled through with the tour before playing some festivals. He played at Summerfest 1996 in Milwaukee, which attracts around 800,000 people each year - this year Alanis Morissette being the opening headliner at the event - before moving onto H.O.R.D.E 1996 through several dates in July. The H.O.R.D.E festival, standing for 'Horizons Of Rock Developing East Coast', was founded in 1992 as a solution for East Coast bands in the US to avoid the club circuit which was sold out in amphitheatres by larger bands. The festival tour was created with initial connections to bands such as Blues Traveller, Grateful Dead and The Spin Doctors.

Lenny said around this time, in connection to the mixed reviews of *Circus* as he travelled on the tour, that he felt music at the time reflected society, that it was cold and had an impersonal sound without soul; he said *his* music was natural and he refused to make a record that did not have heart and soul, something without meaning. He said in interviews his music was as modern as it gets but without the needless technology that drags down much of mainstream music, and he attributed the different reviews of his latest album to the diversity in society's taste. He again had to answer questions on the repeated critique that he takes too much from other artists to create his own sound, his own repertoire, and he answered again with the influence being 'music itself' as opposed to any individual he was trying to replicate. That said, Lenny with *Circus* was again accused of letting his influences dictate his own sound and was reported widely as taking musical aspects of the past and putting them together to make his own. Even though he played down the 'Rock and Roll is Dead' accusation in interviews he widely, and correctly, talked about modern music and the lack of talent. In Germany he spoke of New Orleans and how he loved hanging around in the French Quarter of the city, and he spoke of the music, the history and the talent that was there. He said cab drivers in New Orleans had more talent than anyone in the current charts, and he was probably right.

Other reports during the tour focused on the lack of sales of *Circus*, in particular in the US. Sales at the time were 285,000 compared to the previous 1.9 million of his last record. Again, this was attributed to Lenny remaining within the 1960s/1970s sound he stayed true to; he didn't deviate from his musical riffs, the verbal messages hippie fashion and even the musical equipment of the decade. Lenny was still releasing records in this genre when the mainstream chart was full of hip-hop, rap, alternative rock and computer programmed rhythm and blues. Even live he had comparisons bestowed on him to Led Zeppelin, The Beatles and Jimi Hendrix. The tour itself had the same six piece band and each song was extended to give full throttle to the ensemble. Craig Ross again provided guitar solos with Cindy Blackman flanked behind on drums; she now had her own showcase spot as she blasted her own solo in the middle of 'What Goes Around Comes Around'. Despite it being a brilliant all-round rock show Lenny in some reports simply could not unshackle the constant comparisons to his past influences, both on stage and off. After the remaining shows through the month of August Lenny concluded the *Circus* tour with a concert at the 20,000-seater Coral Sky Amphitheatre at West Palm Beach Florida.

Lenny spent the rest of 1996 and through to 1997 working towards his next album and on this he changed the production and his approach. Maybe this was in response to the critical repetitive rhetoric of his vintage pursuits in sound, or maybe not; either way his next album would have a different production feel to the past. With his fifth album, *5*, Lenny worked with Terry Manning in the studio in pursuit of a more modern sounding album. In the production he embraced digital technology more so than in anything he had previously created and brought in synthesisers and different tape loops which gave the record a more modern sound. The songs he worked through for inclusion still contained more of his 70s-inspired songs with funk and soul, mixed with his rock

56

style, but the production brought a cleaner more contemporary approach to the overall sound.

Terry Manning has a career in music spanning over five decades as an arranger, composer, producer and audio engineer. He had previously engineered ZZ Top's list of multi-platinum albums as well as Led Zeppelin before working with Lenny on 5. Having worked through, written and recorded many songs for the album, Lenny eventually set the release date of May 12th 1998 in the US. It would be an album that would turn into a prolonged extension of commercial success, more so than any previous album he had worked on, and this would be in the main through other external pieces of promotion that pulled it back once again into the charts, from TV, advertisements and film.

Lenny needed an album that would work to expand his worldwide audience and this did just that. It would go on to win him two Grammy Awards. It's an album that established Lenny fully as a genuine funk and R&B artist whilst still maintaining the diversity in his sound. He needed something that would sound different to his past records but still manage to maintain that core fusion he had made his own in soul and rock, a fusion that he was both praised and criticised for in equal measure earlier in his career. After *Circus* he needed an album that would make him more accessible and ultimately this needed to come from the studio and, working alongside Terry Manning, this became the main focus and drive. He succeeded. Lenny emerged at the start of 1998 with a fully accomplished piece of work that offered both new and established Lenny Kravitz followers a different sounding sonic bundle of tunes. He had the balance right, a new sounding record keeping true to his core values and signature compositions.

With 5 Lenny set his sights on returning to some kind of commercial achievement, to have that relevance in a chart system overflowing with talentless non-musicians that he wanted to oust. He had, with his past four albums, achieved tremendous success both on record and also as a mainstream live touring artist, a complete songwriter, musician and multi-instrumentalist. He pursued the in-studio sound techniques to encompass the production in the music the way he wanted it to be heard now, in the present; to modernise the music he had written. He wrote the songs in the same way as before but he was now embracing digital technology and sampling while still keeping true to his core values in sound and studio techniques. He started using Pro Tools, a modern piece of technology first released in 1989. It became the main digital audio workstation and was widely used in sound recording and sound production. It was in fact so widely used that a year later in 1999 the Ricky Martin release 'Livin' la Vida Loca' became the first number one single to be solely recorded, edited, and mixed fully within the Pro Tools environment, so we have that to be thankful for.

At the start of 1998 Lenny felt good about 5; it was an album that he felt worked and he believed he had the balance right, keeping a core Lenny Kravitz feeling on the record but introducing a new modern feel to the production and sound. On its release however, it didn't go to plan. It was a slow start and one that Lenny must have had doubts about as once again the critics would be sharpening their pencils once the album was released. Even more of a disappointment would be the fact that the first three singles released from it didn't bring anything near the chart success many had hoped for.

There must have come a point after the first few months of 5 being out when, watching the first two singles chosen from the album languishing near the edge of the charts, he felt that he had released another *Circus*. Another album that the fans bought and loved but where an opportunity to cross over to mainstream charts was missed. It wouldn't be until the end of the year that 5 would start to be a commercial success; until then Lenny had to watch as once more the critics picked away at his new release, once again complaining that he offered nothing creative, and that all his music was simply replicated from the usual list associated with him. Having worked hard on changing his sound by embracing new technologies with more modern studio techniques Lenny was happy with his new record, and so were his army of fans.

As far as the critics were concerned... well, they could say and write what they wanted, for now, because at the end of the year Lenny would have the last laugh and those same critics who claimed Lenny could no longer write a hit would be silenced, and the criticism would simply *Fly Away*...

Photo © Benédicte Thibaudat

Flying Away

The first single from *5* was 'If You Can't Say No' and was released on April 21st 1998. The music video to the song was directed by Mark Romanek and features model and actress Milla Jovovich throughout. It was a disappointing start to the album, as the single reached number 39 in the USA and 48 in the UK. Around the rest of the world the single reached around the 50 mark and in France it just scraped into the top 100. A month later the album followed, released on May 12th. Sporting a new shorter haircut Lenny kicked off his promotion of his new album with a performance on *David Letterman* on July 20th 1998. He performed the second single scheduled for release, 'Thinking of You', which was written in tribute to his mother, and released on July 6th. It was a relaxed appearance with Lenny in a T-shirt and jeans, no guitar and just singing the vocals. The single had two additional remixes on release, an Emilio Estefan Salsa Version and a Hexum Hip-Hop Remix. It again failed to make any impact onto the main charts around the world, which to some could be viewed as disappointing - hits were what critics were looking at and to some charts were still the go-to place to view whether an act was as popular as they once were or not; but things were changing, and they were changing quickly. The fact was artists like Lenny Kravitz were no longer too concerned with charts and the positioning of singles, and neither were record companies, and looking at what actually filled the charts you can understand why...

It's easy to look at sales of records in the 1990s that didn't have the impact that they had before and instantly conclude the artist is dropping in popularity, especially viewing sales of singles. Expensive music videos in the early to mid-1990s were very common. Michael Jackson had paved the way for these mini movies a decade earlier and it was still a great piece of false theatre to sell a song, but it became less common as it moved onwards through the decade. The reason for this was a simple one: sales of singles did not match or return the cost of making these expensive mini films. Singles were not as popular in the physical sense as they once were, and the record buying public would favour albums over singles. The record industry itself was also changing as media in different forms challenged the conventional chart system; it was becoming ever fragmented and hard to chart in one particular category. Year on year record sales were falling and the singles chart was the main casualty of this. There were some successes that helped boost things here and there: at this time the *Titanic* soundtrack was huge and helped worldwide sales, 'Candle in the Wind' as a charity single by Elton John boosted sales, but apart from these two spikes sales were, year on year, on the decline. Also, these two spikes were helped by factors outside the standard record industry: a soundtrack to a blockbuster movie and a single to commemorate the death of Princess Diana. If these two examples were left to their own devices as purely musical with no external factors it's unlikely they would have had the impact they did. One of the main reasons for this decline was the consumption of different music formats, which was moving fast, and would continue to do so. Musicians like Lenny Kravitz however always had the one advantage over the pop stars of the day who relied heavily on chart positions and record sales - they had the talent to perform live, and the will to tour extensively around the world to stadiums packed with fans who followed them constantly to watch them perform and listen to their music.

This is significant because artists and musicians who had any kind of longevity often found themselves being scrutinised because they didn't sell as many singles as they did before. This was seen by some critics and music writers as a drop in their popularity; they didn't however consider the success when the artist, like Lenny, decided to tour and as a result sold out stadiums around the world. Since its inception in 1955 the popularity of charts and the positions that artists and bands held was the surefire way of determining success and popularity. This remained unchanged for decades on both sides of the pond and now, as we work thorough the 1990s, this system was becoming challenged. Another factor was record contracts themselves as artists, especially forward-thinking ones, were questioning the percentages they made in return for their art, especially when the record company executives were dictating what the artist could or could not release as they searched for a hit above anything else. Prince at this time was the stand-out example of this as an artist challenging the very core of the record contract and searching for other media and platforms to sell his records through; he had at this point in time changed his name to an unpronounceable symbol and was releasing records independently from his contract with Warner Bros. The main purpose of the Hot 100, as it was at the time, was to track the trends of the record buying public. The Billboard system had to change its methods and policies many times to reflect as accurately it could what was actually on trend and popular.

An early count of a single's popularity was that of raw sales and the song's airplay. During the so-called Hot 100's early history singles were the leading way and, in reality, were the only way people bought music. When the singles sales were solid, untouched by any outside influences, more weight was given to a song's retail points than to its radio airplay, but as the decades passed this started to change and the music industry concentrated its efforts more on album sales than singles. Musicians and artists started to create more albums and concentrate their efforts on this as a whole and not be too concerned with singles; this was where they expressed their creativity. Lenny's first two singles released from 5 came at a time when record companies, Virgin in this case, were starting to consider not releasing singles at all as a song's actual airplay was weighted more than its sales. Over the years Billboard has adjusted the sales vs airplay ratio many times to try and predict and reflect the true popularity of songs. Lenny's two singles released at the start of 5 both contained no B-sides or additional tracks and considering his songwriting ability this must have been a conscious decision, as he would have had countless songs sitting around that he could have offered as additional tracks. It was just the song itself on the first single and on the second single a couple of remixes. Many artists were doing the same as talented musicians such as Lenny poured their efforts into albums of complete music without the distraction of looking for so-called single hits.

5 was recorded at Ghetto Lounge Studios in New York and Compass Point Studios in the Bahamas. In 1992 Terry Manning had taken over all aspects of Compass Point Studios, restoring and rewiring it to make it modernised for the future, as it was previously in a state of decline and in need of an upgrade. Although Lenny had modernised his sound on 5 he still stayed true to his core writing. 'Live' was co-written with Craig Ross and goes for the straight rock and funk approach; it has a lot going on within the song including a brass section and a long saxophone lead by Harold Todd towards the end of the opening track: it sets the tone perfectly for what's to come. The second track, the aptly named 'Supersoulfighter', finds Kravitz fully involved in the theme; here he gives synths in the style of soul and provides sound effects over a pounding drum beat - it's a song that sounds like it was made to perform live and add to the touring ammunition. 'I Belong to You' stays in familiar territory for Lenny and although it's a good solid album track it doesn't stretch far and has little variation. Comparisons were made again to Bowie on the vocal delivery of 'Black Velveteen' and 'If You Can't Say No' returns back to Lenny in R&B mode layering keyboards, piano and organ; it's a track made for singing and suits Lenny's vocals perfectly; it was also the tribute song to Lenny's mother. The next track, 'Take Time', was again heavily compared to Prince in its overall feel and sound. The second half of the album only gets better, full of funk and soul and musically diverse from track to track. 'Fly Away' kicks things off, yet to be the big smash it later turned into, for now staying smugly within the album waiting for its big break. After 'Fly Away' comes the excellent 'It's Your Life' - here Lenny lays on another heavy funk rock tune embellished with synth horns and melodic verses over a pointed bass line. 'Straight Cold Player' has Cindy Blackman back on drums and the tune is driven by her beat; 'Little Girl's Eyes' is a slow soul ballad again using synth for an atmosphere; it has a long outro and a classy guitar lead. On the original release of 5 there were also two more superb tracks. The guitar-led 'You're My Flavor' has another Beatles type feel and

63

again Lenny's vocals are superb on the track. The final track on the original release 'Can We Find a Reason?' is an acoustic track with heavy Hammond organ; it has a gospel feel and is soulful throughout; it finishes the album completely and on a straight listen completes an outstanding collection of songs which touch, hint and at times smash straight through all of Lenny's influences.

After the *David Letterman Show* Lenny played a few shows in Europe before touring again in the USA. He played in Seattle and Los Angeles throughout the end of September 1998 before heading across to Las Vegas, Dallas, Texas, Houston on September 27th and then Nashville. Again, the concerts were both visually and performance-wise superb with Lenny now adding in his new material to his sets. He finished the tour in October with shows in Boston, New York, Atlanta and Florida where he played a set at The House of Blues Lake Buena Vista before he headed for Europe. Before this however Lenny was featured in a spot of voiceover work. On November 20th 1998 *The Rugrats Movie* was released, featuring Lenny as a baby singer in the movie, which also had Iggy Pop and Patti Smith amongst others, also as baby singers. The movie starred Cree Summer as one of the main voices, who Lenny would collaborate with over the coming months on her album which was released in 1999.

Lenny kicked off in Europe with a concert in Germany before heading to the Netherlands and then England, this time back at Brixton Academy for a show on December 7th. A typical show from this tour started with a Radio Edit before going straight into new opener 'Live', then the following: 'It Ain't Over 'Till It's Over', 'Always on the Run', 'Mr Cab Driver', 'Are You Gonna Go My Way', 'American Woman', 'Fly Away', 'Radio Outro'. Lenny then returned for additional tracks, encores, 'Let Love Rule' etc... And as before the set changed slightly as the tour progressed, depending on where he was. When the tour returned to France for example Lenny had changed the intro to the concerts; here he started with 'Whole Lotta Love' before moving into 'Straight Cold Player' and then 'Live'. Lenny played Belgium on December 8th at National Forest before playing back in Germany, France, Italy and Austria. Lenny concluded the European tour back in Germany with a concert in Stuttgart on December 22nd.

The tour as always for Lenny was successful and lucrative, and as with all great musicians and performers this was where the real success lay. The charts were not as vital as they once were, as I have previously discussed, and artists like Lenny saw the touring and the albums as their core indicator. On this basis after another sell out European tour Lenny Kravitz was as successful a live act as you could get and his albums reached the people that mattered, his hardcore huge following. That said, a very surprising leap in popularity was about to happen as Lenny released the third single from 5. Third singles are third singles for a reason, not as important as the first two, and by the time a third single is released an album has been out for a while, sometimes months, and so the public who bought the album already have the track. Unless there's a significant EP or extra tracks included then there really would be no point buying it unless you have it just to collect, so sales of third singles are naturally lower than the first two; but not for Lenny on 5. This standard third single trend was about to change, and change big style - his third release would be one of the biggest hits he would have, and one of the biggest over his entire career.

The track 'Fly Away' sat happily on 5 without any real fanfare; it's a catchy melody with a prominent slap bass over a solid beat. It was originally recorded as a ballad but Lenny revised the track and gave it the funk treatment. The track was completed very quickly, after the album was already finished, with Lenny originally intending it to be a B-side only. After hearing the song again however Lenny called his record company and stopped the whole procedure and added the song to the album. It was a good move. As stated before singles did not have the instant potential for sales they once had: other factors needed to come into play across other aspects of the media to help boost any popularity. Previously in the 1980s artists and bands could rely on the singles alone, to a degree, as the promotional activity of the record company, and radio and TV appearances were more than enough to get the single into homes and onto the buying public. There were only a few channels on TV so it was easy to capture a huge audience through TV and radio to promote a single. Now in 1998/1999 a full cross media strategy was required; sometimes this was planned and sometimes a particular tune was picked up and instantly had an increase in exposure. A single alone through a standard release was no longer reaching people through traditional means, no matter how good or commercial it was, full cross media was what was required and fortunately for Lenny this is exactly what happened with 'Fly Away'. The lyrics are very simple, and the song kicks in instantly and this makes it perfect for TV and advertisements that have a limited time to get their message across; it's an ideal stand-out track for sports montages and movie scenes where there is no deep meaning trying to be conveyed. Lenny created a monster song that fits this aspect as well as keeping it simple with basic ideas that still worked together.

As a result 'Fly Away' was chosen as a tune for commercials for Southwest Airlines, who ran their advertising campaign through 1998 and beyond, and in addition MSN and the Peugeot 206 used it in their commercials. It was also showcased for the first Nissan Xterra advertisements. The momentum carried on over the month when it was also featured in the film *Coyote Ugly*, and became the theme song for the Canadian reality television series *Ice Pilots NWT*. Another trailer followed when it was used in the Comic Con trailer for *Star Trek Discovery* season two and later in the 1999 NBA Finals broadcaster NBC used it for their montage. Even newly formed 'Internet personalities' picked up on the track using it with altered lyrics for various montages and clips.

The above led to a huge leap in popularity as the song became used across many different platforms across the media; with its instantly recognisable intro and with Lenny's distinctive vocals it became, at the end of 1998 and into 1999, a huge success. It was eventually released on December 29th 1998 and went on to be massive hit for Lenny. The single went to number one in the UK and rose to 12 in the USA on Billboard; it also topped the mainstream rock charts and the modern rock charts and many others in the increasingly fragmented chart system. It remained in the charts all through 1999 as well, and charted all over the world due to the ongoing increase in its exposure. Directed this time by Paul Hunter the video for the single shows Lenny playing the track in a club surrounded by partygoers, with some of them getting hot and steamier through the song. The video was edited afterwards to make it look grainy and beat up for the illusion of an old tape, or a discovery from the past. The album, on the back on the single, suddenly became reenergised and sales started to increase, as did interest in Lenny's back catalogue. There were 2 CDs available for the single, the first with the main track followed by a live acoustic version including 'Believe', also acoustic; this was also the version released in the UK. The second CD had the single version, the extended album version and a B-side 'Call Out Hook'.

Still on tour Lenny continued on the back of the success of the 'Fly Away' single through the US. He played a concert at the Fox Theatre in Atlanta before the 41st Grammy Awards was held on 24th February 1999 in Los Angeles. Lenny won The Best Rock Vocal Award for 'Fly Away' at the ceremony. Continuing on, Lenny travelled to Canada playing Toronto and Montreal for concerts on March 10th and 11th, then played four dates through California in April with 'Fly Away' now closing the concerts.

While touring Lenny continued with his collaborations when he worked with American singer and actress Cree Summer, who he had previously featured alongside him on *The Rugrats Movie*. Cree released her first full length album *Street Faerie* on April 20th 1999. Lenny produced the record and appeared throughout. Earlier, in 1993, Cree had completed an album with her band Subject To Change through Capital Records as the lead singer, but the label didn't officially release it and it was only made available through promotional activity. The band itself performed regularly and held strong political messages; they became a popular support act touring alongside other bands. Produced by Lenny, *Street Faërie* only achieved moderate success in the US. It was Cree Summer's first full length album in her own name away from her band. Cree toured and supported Lenny on his own tour in promotion of the record and even though she went down well with the audiences the label eventually decided to drop her; in addition she was also due to perform at Lilith Fair but this was also subsequently cancelled. Lilith Fair was a tour and travelling music festival initially founded by the Canadian musician Sarah McLachlan, Nettwerk Music Group's Dan Fraser and Terry McBride; it also had a connection with New York talent agent Marty Diamond. It took place initially during the summers of 1997 to 1999 and was later brought back for the summer of 2010. It consisted solely of female solo artists and female-led bands and in its initial three years raised over $10m for charity. Work Group, which at the time was an imprint of Sony Music, claimed they dropped Cree Summer for creative differences that they couldn't resolve but although she was dropped from the label they did however continue to promote and market the album by sending out a four-track sampler to radio stations. This also included a remix of the track 'Revelation Sunshine' which they made available in Europe. There was also a version which unusually was only made available for Austria. Lyrically the album explores many themes covering spirituality, racism and romance. Cree Summer went on to become a popular voice actress featuring in many animated films including *The Rugrats Movie* with Lenny, *Clifford the Big Red Dog*, *Tiny Tunes Adventures* and many more.

Lenny's tour now started to take on more prominence as *5* started to regain momentum. It had reached a decent standing but hadn't really made a massive impact; now with the release on 'Fly Away' it was given an injection and started to rise again through the ever-changing fragmented chart system and general popularity. He played 19 full concerts through the month of May 1999 to sold out arenas through the US, starting in San Antonio on May 1st and ending the month at the 17,500 capacity PNC Banks Arts Centre in New Jersey.

As June came around another injection would propel *5* even further forward: again another cross media venture saw Lenny top the charts and rise further to the top of the tree. Lenny recorded a cover song for a new movie about to be released that would appear on the soundtrack. *Austin Powers: The Spy Who Shagged Me* was the second film in the Austin Powers series starring Mike Myers. Lenny recorded a cover of 'American Woman' originally recorded and released by Guess Who in January 1970; the original went on to be number one on the Billboard Hot 100, and Lenny's revival of the track also went on to be a huge success.

The film and soundtrack were both released on June 1st 1999. The movie itself was directed by Jay Roach who also directed the first instalment of the Austin Powers series, *International Man of Mystery*, in 1997. This second instalment has

68

Mike Myers, who incidentally is the franchise co-producer and writer, playing Austin Powers himself, Dr. Evil, and a new character, the charming 'Fat Bastard'. The film also has many other stars and guest appearances including Heather Graham, Michael York, Robert Wagner, Seth Green, and Elizabeth Hurley. Again, the film follows on in the James Bond spoof arena with the title playing on *The Spy Who Loved Me* from 1977. The movie itself was hugely successful and grossed around $312 million in worldwide ticket sales; in fact in its first weekend alone it took in more money than the total amount of the first film at the box office. The soundtrack for the film was also extremely successful and this was due to the film being heavily influenced by the music within it. There are many soundtracks to movies but what made the Austin Powers movies successful musically was the fact that they are tinged with the 60s and 70s style that made the decades so popular, and this made it relevant, cool, and retro for the present day. The music within the film was extremely important and, although it wasn't a musical film in the true sense of what a musical film should be, the accompanying soundtrack was a focal point to the overall feeling of the movie. The soundtrack itself also had a list of collaborators that made the film even more popular: it featured Madonna, The Who, R.E.M, Green Day, Burt Bacharach, Quincy Jones and many more, including Lenny. The soundtrack was released on Madonna's label Maverick, which was launched seven years earlier in April 1992.

Maverick was a collaborative enterprise between Madonna herself, Frederick DeMann, Veronica Ronnie Dashev and the Time Warner group. The name is a combination of the three founders Madonna, Veronica and Frederick. At the time of the soundtrack's release Maverick had divisions covering recording, music publishing, television, film, merchandising and book publishing. Maverick was part of a new deal that Madonna had signed with Time Warner which was reported at the time to be worth $60 million. It encompassed recordings of her own songs as well as the label she had set up. The deal also reportedly allowed her to achieve 20% royalties from the music proceeds which at the time was one of the highest rates in the industry. This was widely reported as Michael Jackson and Prince were also negotiating large contracts around this time and the three were in the press heavily, as the three biggest stars in the world negotiated deals that could set a precedent for others going forward. The first releases for Maverick as a new label would be Madonna's 1992 coffee table publication *Sex* alongside her studio album *Erotica*, which as expected at the time came with an incredible amount of criticism and controversy in light of the contents and subject matter. *Erotica* followed on the theme that Lenny had installed with 'Justify my Love'; this controversy didn't last long however and soon the label would introduce a huge breakthrough act when it signed a rising star who had just recorded her third album and had just signed to Maverick. The album would become one of the best-selling albums of the entire decade, in fact it was an absolute monster and of course the label benefited tremendously from it. In 1995 Alanis Morissette released her third album *Jagged Little Pill*, which went on to be certified an incredible 16x platinum in America and achieved an additional $33 million in worldwide sales. This made it the biggest selling album in the label's history, and one of the biggest selling of the entire 1990s and beyond.

The first single from the Austin Powers soundtrack was from Madonna herself, who released 'Beautiful Stranger' on the 29th May, a day before the release of the film. The video features Austin Powers throughout gazing up at Madonna as she performs the track on stage; it's a fantastic advert for the movie and set the scene perfectly. The track was co-written and co-produced by Madonna with William Orbit, whom she had collaborated with on her album *Ray of Light*. There were many different mixes of the single released in various forms making it a stand-out dance track and extremely radio friendly; naturally it was a huge hit all over the world and made the movie and the soundtrack instantly popular. Less successful was the second single from the soundtrack, an awful cover of Cameo's 'Word Up' by Mel G of The Spice Girls, later to be known as Mel B.

Lenny's version of 'American Woman' was released as the third single in June 1999 and earned him more chart success around the world, and eventually another Grammy award. It's a slightly softer cover than the original and doesn't have the guitar solo. Lenny later said that he couldn't get the sound he wanted for the solo so decided to leave it off. The video for the song was directed by Paul Hunter who had directed many music videos for a variety of artist including Pharell, Dr Dre, Beyonce, Justin Timberlake and Michael Jackson. The video featured Heather Graham throughout as well as many other close up shots of women riding motorcycles and dancing in front of Lenny as he performs on stage in front of the American Stars and Stripes, Springsteen style. The single released came with several B-sides, 'American Woman' as a single version, a live version of 'Straight Cold Player', a remix of 'Thinking of You' and a live performance of 'Fields of Joy'.

Riding on the back of the 'Fly Away' single and now with 'American Woman' successfully charting around the world, 5 was reissued to include it as an additional track. The reissue also included another track, 'Without You', which made the new release a 15-track album where the original had 13 tracks. The reissue instantly gave the album a fresh boost and it remained in the charts around the world for nearly three years. Lenny was initially criticised for sounding unoriginal and lifting ideas from others as a reason for underperforming in the charts but now things had changed. 'Fly Away' was still being played everywhere, picked up for advertising and promotions by various large companies with its perfect intro, making it instantly recognisable. In addition, a major blockbuster movie had utilised Lenny's cover of 'American Woman' and this made the record buying public purchase 5 in earnest, and it became one of the bestselling albums of 1999, putting Lenny straight back to the top of the various charts on the back of the two singles. On the back of this incredible uplift he continued his tour, now heading to Europe once more in June 1999.

The European leg kicked off in Germany on June 13th 1999 before a concert in Vienna, which was followed by a festival appearance at Steel City Festival in Linz. He played Wembley Stadium on June 26th before playing a set at the Glastonbury festival on June 27th alongside Skunk Anansie, and then played Paris and the Netherlands before returning to Germany on July 3rd. The set for the European leg remained similar to that in the US: the concert usually started with 'Is There Any Love in Your Heart' followed by 'Live', 'It Ain't Over 'Till It's Over',

'Supersoulfighter', Blues for Sister Someone', 'Tunnel Vision' and 'American Woman'. The second half of the show would start with 'Fields of Joy' followed by 'Always on the Run', 'Freedom Train', 'Rock and Roll is Dead', 'Be', 'Let Love Rule' and then 'Fly Away' and 'Are You Gonna Go My Way' as an encore. After a concert in Belgium Lenny played in Spain with two sell out concerts on July 7th and 8th before concluding the European leg of the tour on July 17th 1999. He was still huge in Europe and the two singles alongside the reissue of 5 meant that all Lenny's concerts in Europe were sold out; the demand was exceptional and forced Lenny to often return to countries as demand grew further. His love affair with European audiences from the start was greater than that of the US and now, even though he was gaining popularity in America and charting high, the European standing was still higher at this time. Whenever Lenny toured Europe the concerts were always at capacity and the crowds loved him.

He returned to the USA and continued through North America starting in Minneapolis on August 25th before heading into Canada. While there Lenny played at The MuchMusic Video Awards where he played 'American Woman' and was joined on stage by Burton Cummings and Randy Bachman from the original Guess Who. Lenny received great praise for the performance, which was superb, and also for acknowledging the originators. Florida followed, with two concerts on September 24th and 25th before he played in New Orleans at Lakefront Arena on September 28th. Lenny played all through October on the tour, playing to sell out crowds in Dallas, Albuquerque, California, Seattle and again in Florida where he played at Citrus Bowl on October 30th. He performed again shortly after at the Z100 Jingle Ball celebrations at Madison Square Garden, others on the bill including Enrique Iglesias, Ricky Martin, Jessica Simpson and Jennifer Lopez, which took place on December 16th.

After the Madison Square Garden event Lenny travelled back to the Bahamas to relax and reflect on the past year, which had been one that had propelled him back into the mainstream of popularity. It was while he was here however that he received a phone call from Prince, who was holding a pay per view concert to be broadcast on New Year's Eve, and Prince wanted Lenny to guest with him onstage; and as it was Prince, he couldn't say no. Lenny took a flight to Minneapolis where after virtually no sleep he arrived at Paisley Park, the home studio complex of Prince. The complex also housed a full soundstage where Prince would perform full concerts frequently and with the crowd waiting Lenny got the nod at close to midnight and went straight on stage. He performed 'Fly Away' and 'American Woman' with Prince alongside. The show, entitled Rave Unto the Year 2000, was a promotional concert for Prince's new album *Rave Unto the Joy Fantastic* which featured collaborations with Sheryl Crow, Gwen Stefani and others.

Also, in December 1999 another key influence often cited in connection with Lenny's songs died. On 26th December Curtis Mayfield died from complications of type 2 diabetes after a tragic accident nine years earlier on August 13th 1990. While at an outdoor event concert at Wingate Field in Flatbush Brooklyn New York stage equipment fell on him, the accident leaving him paralysed from the neck down. Afterwards, even though he was unable to play guitar, he still continued to compose music and to sing, his vocals being recorded line-by-line while he was lying on his back. Curtis Mayfield was one of the most influential musicians behind soul; his music was heavily politically and drove the 'black freedom' 'black movement' message, as it was as the time, through the very core of the writing. His sound, the way he produced his records and of course his voice was often described within Lenny's work; in fact it would be difficult for anyone moving anywhere near this genre, whether that be musically or lyrically, without being compared to and influenced by Curtis Mayfield.

1999 had been a sort of breakthrough year for Lenny. He had the previous year released an album that embraced digital technology and moved him away, from a production point of view, from his old techniques. Initially 5 received only mediocre reviews, not that it mattered, and it took a slow and steady process for it to achieve worldwide success. The hits came through slowly at first, 'I Belong to You' and then the breakthrough of 'Fly Away' which made the album stand out from the crowd. Later 'American Woman' made this even more prominent and led to a reissue with an additional track. All of this led to the album becoming Lenny's most successful studio album to date. It was the album to establish his career at a higher level and give him increasing worldwide popularity, especially in Europe. It won him his first two Grammy Awards and of course with the addition of Lenny's constant touring it became a year that he rose to the top. As the year closed he was well established as a brilliant live performer with a growing back catalogue of quality material. Even though *5* looked like it would initially be another album that didn't quite make it through, especially in an ever-changing fast-moving chart system that favoured far less talented individuals and bands, the album when reissued had a new lease of life. *5* was Lenny's strongest album to date and now it was time to reflect, it was time to demonstrate to the masses that he had a full track list of hits that was would be worthy of a Greatest Hits compilation. With *5* Lenny had proved that rock and roll was in fact very much *alive…*

Photo © Romain Pasquini

Photo © Laurent Valay

Diggin In

Lenny kicked off the new millennium with a performance at The American Music Awards on January 17th 2000. He performed 'American Woman' at the event. He returned to the studio through February and March before playing three shows in South Africa, playing a sold-out concert at The Johannesburg Stadium on March 17th followed by Kings Park Stadium in Durban and finally a show at Green Point Stadium in Cape Town. The Johannesburg concert however received a different headline to most of Lenny's shows: seven gunmen stole nearly half a million rand, around $36,000, in takings from refreshments sold at the Friday night concert. It was reported at the time that they stole them from the stalls. A police spokesman said that the men held up a manager and employees at the company with the refreshment stalls contract early on the Saturday morning as they were counting the money in an office inside the stadium after Lenny had performed. They also stole a computer and phones. It wasn't reported if Lenny and the band lost out financially from the raid but as this was a refreshment contract it is doubtful he would have been affected.

In May Lenny played at the SunFest music and art festival which is held annually on the first week of May in West Palm Beach Florida. The event had been going since 1982 and was still just as popular year on year. It's the state's largest waterfront festival and attracts around 275,000 visitors with three main stages showcasing a wide and diverse array of musical styles from jazz right across the spectrum to hip-hop. Lenny played his set on May 3rd and as usual a large crowd gathered to see him perform. Shortly after on the 5th of May Lenny played the 7,800-seater Municipal Auditorium in New Orleans. The set list now had a familiar run through starting with 'Live', then onto 'Supersoulfighter', 'Tunnel

Vision', 'Stop Draggin Around', 'Fields Of Joy', 'Always on the Run' with a drum solo, 'Let Love Rule', 'American Woman', 'Fly Away' and ending with 'Are You Gonna Go My Way'. The following night still in New Orleans Lenny played a similar set at The New Orleans Jazz and Heritage Festival 2000 at Fair Grounds Racecourse. This event had been long established and was first held back in 1970, primarily an annual celebration of the music and culture of New Orleans and Louisiana with the term Jazz Fest referring to the days in and around the festival; with this being New Orleans there were many unaffiliated New Orleans bars and nightclubs that held musical events during the festival weekends so the whole city and surrounding areas became a celebration of music.

A week later, on 13th May, Lenny and the band played at Wango Tango, the annual day-long concert produced by local Los Angeles radio station KIIS-FM. The series of concerts had been staged at various venues around southern California including the Dodger Stadium in Los Angeles, the Rose Bowl in Pasadena, Angel Stadium in Anaheim, Verizon Wireless Amphitheatre in Irvine, Staples Centre in Los Angeles and the StubHub Centre. The concert series is noted for featuring several marquee performers in a day-long series of sets; usually celebrities are in attendance and introduce each act. Lenny played his set which this year was held at the Dodger stadium, the home of baseball team the Los Angeles Dodgers, a venue that held 56,000 people.

Lenny stayed in LA for the remainder of the month before playing his own stand-alone concert again at the Dodger Stadium on May 30th before Miami at the 21,000-seater newly built American Airlines Arena for a concert in July. On September 21st Lenny appeared at The MuchMusic Video Awards in Toronto, where he played 'American Woman' again with Guess Who at the event. Performing this year as well as Lenny were Barenaked Ladies, Moby, Destiny's Child and Blink 182.

On the back of all the recent success both in the charts and on tour Lenny now started to put together the final touches to his new album, a greatest hits collection. Lenny was at a career high and 5 had exceeded all expectations: it was still high in the charts all over the world and with Lenny's constant touring and with his level of performing brilliant sell out shows it looked like it would continue to remain there for years to come. A greatest hits package could only reaffirm his status as a truly great rock star, and it would also demonstrate his truly impressive back catalogue of material and add more to his reputation as an incredible performer and songwriter. Lenny performed in October on *The Late Show with David Letterman*, *Saturday Night Live* and *The Tonight Show with Jay Leno* prior to the release of his *Greatest Hits* package.

Released on October 24th 2000 and spanning his career from 1988-2000, the album covered all Lenny's past releases. The material grouped together in this way showcased Lenny in all his various forms. It was of course instantly referenced as not original but it was still uniquely fresh in its overall feel and this was mainly due to the brilliance in the studio to bring all his influences together. The album showed Lenny's early career and the changes along the way as he moved into guitar based stadium rock, and one thing Lenny Kravitz always had was a knack of securing singles that were instantly catchy to the ear and memorable for the listener. The album is a fantastic musical cocoon of the peak of Lenny's talents so far, even if the sequencing is out, and it also featured his new single 'Again' which was the only new song on the *Greatest Hits* album. The song was originally intended for an album of original songs, but Lenny felt it didn't fit the tone of the particular album and allowed it to be released with his *Greatest Hits*, which was a good choice. It won the 2000 Grammy for Best Male Rock Vocal Performance. Lenny won the same award in 1998 and 1999 for 'Fly Away' and 'American Woman' and he made it four in a row when he won the next year for 'Dig In'. The collection listed the following on the original release: 'Are You Gonna Go My Way', 'Fly Away', 'Rock and Roll Is Dead', 'Again', 'It Ain't Over 'Till It's Over', 'Can't Get You Off My Mind', 'Mr. Cab Driver', 'American Woman', 'Stand by My Woman', 'Always on the Run', 'Heaven Help', 'I Belong to You', 'Believe', 'Let Love Rule', and finally 'Black Velveteen'. The Japanese edition had 'Is There Any Love in Your Heart' as track 12, the rest of the album remaining the same.

Despite the usual critics saying the same thing in connection to Lenny's influences within his songs, with the usual references to Prince, Hendrix and Zeppelin, one thing this album demonstrated was that Lenny was a *blend* of his influences: he unashamedly intertwined them into his songs, and more to the point he openly celebrated it. The album is a mix of all of Lenny's past work and stands as a great example of what he was all about to this point - every musical style available is explored, celebrated, and ultimately, delivered. The compilation came with a booklet and just to prove Lenny's modesty and shyness it contained 20 pages of himself, and in various stages of undress; this was a shame as it could have served as a great opportunity to add a small bio on the creation of each track, and also to acknowledge others involved in the recordings. The record company however were moving to capitalise on Lenny and his increasing popularity on the back of *5*, and on reflection looking at the sales of the compilation on release, they were right to do so. The collection sold over 10 million copies worldwide and he gained another huge hit when the single and new track written for the album reached number 4 on the Billboard Hot 100 Singles chart. The single came with a video showing a storyboard type scenario with Lenny and his on-screen video girlfriend; it also has shots of concert scenes as the video progresses and a scene of Lenny undressing and taking a shower, just for good measure. It went platinum in Austria, France, the Netherlands, Norway, Poland, Switzerland and the UK, and it went 2x platinum in Argentina, Spain, Germany and Australia, and it went 3x platinum in Belgium and crucially the US where it sold just under 4 million copies. The album was revised and updated later in 2005 to include his latest albums at the time, *Lenny* and *Baptism* respectively. With any greatest hits package there is also a natural surge in the standard back catalogue, which also happened, so the release of the compilation pushed Lenny even further into the mainstream.

With his *Greatest Hits* package flying high in the charts Lenny spent time through the year recording in Miami, when he wasn't working alongside or contributing his talent to others, compiling what would be his next album. Things were going very well, *5* still hung around the charts and the *Greatest Hits* collection was still selling very well, keeping him in the public eye. Lenny, again with his collaborators in the studio of Henry Hirsch, Craig

Ross and David Baron on string arrangements, worked through his demos and completed his track listing, sitting at 13 new songs. As we were now on first name terms, he decided on the new release to be called simply *Lenny* and it was scheduled for release in October. It would be his 6th studio album so far and he now released his first single for the record on August 13th 2001, the album track and first single 'Dig In'.

'Dig In', like 'Fly Away', benefited from being picked up in various promotional campaigns. It was used in promos by the National Basketball Association for the 2002 NBA playoffs, and it was utilised in the movie *Returner* as the ending theme to the film; the movie was huge in Japan and was heavily promoted. The single came with additional tracks, 'Rosemary' and a live performance of 'Can't Get You Off My Mind'. 'Dig In' became a huge hit in the US for Lenny: it rose through the charts and eventually became one of the most successful songs he released. In Europe it was equally as huge and dominated the charts.

The video for the single was directed by Samuel Bayer, who had directed the 'Black Velveteen' video from *5* previously. It shows a program on TV similar to QVC which morphs into Lenny and the band performing in the middle of the sea, off the coast of Miami, surrounded by a helicopter. The video has layers of special effects giving the impression it has speed and tracking issues. The video itself was originally planned to be shot at the top of the Empire State Building on September 12, 2001 but the terrorist attacks on the World Trade Centre the day before caused the location to be moved. The track also would go on to earn Lenny his fourth consecutive Grammy Award, for Best Male Rock Vocal Performance, a year later, for his performance on the song.

After the *Greatest Hits* compilation album release, and now with 'Dig In' sitting high in the charts, more kudos was about to come Lenny's way. Another major star was about to release a solo album that Lenny had contributed to. Michael Jackson released his album *Invincible* on October 30th 2001. It would be Michael's last recording released before his death in 2009, and the release coincidentally would be the same date Lenny planned to release his next album. Lenny worked with Michael and co-wrote the track '(I Can't Make It) Another Day'; however, the track was dropped from the album and was never used. Later on, on January 2nd 2010, the song was leaked onto the internet. It was just 90 seconds long, and was referred to as 'Another Day'. The leak features the vocals of Michael Jackson and Lenny cannot be heard, but Lenny was later confirmed to be present, and it was confirmed as a duet between the two. Although Lenny initially was not attributed to the song after the leak to the internet, he confirmed he had indeed composed and produced it. He also denied he had personally leaked the track but stated at the time that he would like to have the track officially released in full someday. Shortly after the leak was broadcast both Jackson's estate and the record label, Sony Music Entertainment, tried to remove the track from the internet altogether for copyright reasons. They initially succeeded but the song continued to be re-uploaded and, despite multiple efforts, it was listened to and uploaded thousands of times. Lenny himself later reworked the track and gave it a new name, 'Storm', and it became a collaboration between Lenny and rapper Jay-Z and went on to be featured on *Baptism* in 2004.

Lenny also worked through 2001 with the Red Hot Organisation which, in conjunction with Amazon.com, founded the charity to increase awareness in the public of AIDS. It fought AIDS through various avenues within pop culture and featured rare memorabilia including the work of Rolling Stone photographer Mark Seliger who worked with Lenny on a photo book to be released in November. The charity started in 1989 and over 400 artists contributed to over 15 compilation albums, including producers and directors. There were also TV and media events to raise donations for the cause, and the charity raised over 10 million dollars for the cause for HIV/AIDS relief around the world. Many of the charity albums were in tribute to a particular artist, and there was in this instance a trio of albums released with Lenny featuring on the third. It was called *Red Hot + Indigo* and is the thirteenth entry from the Red Hot AIDS benefit series of compilation albums produced by Paul Heck. It marks the tenth anniversary of the Red Hot Organisation and is in tribute to jazz legend Duke Ellington.

Lenny was released on October 30th 2001 with 'Dig In' still riding high in the charts around the world. Recorded in Miami, the album gave Lenny songwriting comparisons to George Michael

81

and Prince, that of writing, arranging, producing and performing on every song on the album, making it a truly solo affair and keeping the minimal sound. It also featured live percussion and drum programming. There are some interesting songs on the album that also reflect some personal issues Lenny had encountered; one stand-out track in relation to past events was 'Bank Robber Man' which was written about a real incident that Lenny was involved in when he was accidentally mistaken for a criminal and arrested by the Miami police. The arresting officers didn't believe he was in fact Lenny Kravitz and because he had no form of ID he had to wait, in handcuffs, until he was eventually cleared. One thing that was reoccurring in reviews of the album *Lenny* was it was consistent in strength: there are no real weak tracks on the album, it's a class weave of all of the tenacity Lenny Kravitz brings to his albums again showing his unapologetic classic rock influences and his devotion in recreating them. It's another electric blend with spiritual lyrics, it's raw and uncomplicated and on ground that Lenny is now more that comfortable with, and it's an album that once again can add songs to his live repertoire. The album has a great feel to it and it's a statement once again that Lenny was unique in his re-creation of his past influences, a style that he again was criticised for by some but this is what made him unique, and once again it was nothing but excellent music, written in an age when these kinds of songs and the craft involved in creating them were becoming increasingly rare. Releasing the single 'Again' was a masterful move ahead of the album, and the single was widely regarded as one of his best, and the following release of 'Dig In' and now the actual album kept the momentum in full spin. It's a studio craft that Lenny was now renowned for, culminating in songs of classic homages to rock; it's also heavily melodic throughout and the balance and feel of the album is completely synchronised. With *Lenny* the album, he now had once and for all demonstrated his own musical signature - his influences no longer mattered, it was boring to try and spot them because this was what Lenny Kravitz did, and on *Lenny* he did it better than anyone.

More collaborations followed a month after the release of *Lenny* when on November 19th 2001 Mick Jagger, who Lenny had previously worked with on the track 'Use Me' on Mick's solo album *Wandering Spirit*, released his fourth solo album *Goddess in the Doorway*, his first release with Virgin Records. It followed on from the successful *Voodoo Lounge* and *Bridges to Babylon* released by the Stones in 1994 and 1997. Mick started the project in 2000 and once he had enough material started work in the studio around March/April 2001. Primarily Mick worked alongside other people in collaboration of his album, notably Marti Frederiksen and Matt Clifford as producers; he enlisted many musicians for the album recording including the talents of Lenny to assist on tracks. The sessions themselves were filmed for a documentary entitled *Being Mick* which showcased the recording process for the album; it was a film that followed Mick Jagger for an entire year though the creative process of the making of *Goddess in the Doorway* featuring studio work, travelling, family life, his friends, and touring. It has an almost amateur feeling to it as much of the footage was filmed by Mick using a handheld camera. Also featured in the film are Mick attending an Elton John charity fundraiser and the premiere of the movie *Enigma*, starring Kate Winslet, which Jagger's company produced. *Being Mick* was directed by Kevin Macdonald and Jim Gable and received its debut on television on the channel ABC, the DVD of the movie being released in May 2002 through Lionsgate Home Entertainment. At the end of the summer the album featuring Lenny, and featuring him in the studio with Mick in the movie, was completed. 'God Gave Me Everything' was produced by Lenny and he was heavily featured on the track, and it was put forward as the lead single in October 2001. 'God Gave Me Everything' was the fourth track on the album and has a driving riff very much in the style of The Rolling Stones. The single did moderately well and peaked at number 24 on the mainstream charts; the album itself however did very well and was critically acclaimed. Mick received some of the strongest reviews of his entire career. Not everyone however liked *Goddess in the Doorway*: Keith Richards, in his own unique way, decided to rename the album 'Dogshit in the Doorway'.

In November 2001 Lenny released a photo book of himself, naturally, created by Mark Seliger whose work was featured in The Red Hot Organisation charity for AIDS/HIV awareness. The book has pictures of Lenny on tour as well as with his friends and family;

it also shows many photographs of Lenny in various posed portraits.

Lenny closed off 2001 with a performance at My VH1 Music Awards in Los Angeles on December 2nd. He arrived on the red carpet looking like the true rock star, wearing his trademark glasses, flared jeans and knitted hat with a long knitted coat dragging behind him, bare chest and full feathers around his shoulders. Also performing at the awards were Sting, the aforementioned Mick Jagger and Mary J.Blige.

On 29th January 2002 the second single from the album *Lenny* was released, 'Stillness of Heart', co-written with Craig Ross. The single came with an acoustic version and 'Flowers for Zoe', again as an acoustic. The single charted reasonably well reaching 38 in the US, on the US Modern Chart, and mid 40s in the UK. It also reached similar positions around Europe and the rest of the world.

In March Lenny headed to Europe where he played in Germany and the Netherlands at The Amuse on March 8th. In April he returned to New Orleans and played once again at The New Orleans Jazz and Heritage Festival at Fair Grounds Race Course; added to the sets this time were 'Stillness of Heart' and 'Yesterday is Gone'. Lenny returned to New York in May for a set at Hammerstein Ballroom on May 3rd before returning once again to Germany. He started off by playing Rock am Ring 2002 in Nürburgring, Nürburg. The festival is held annually over two consecutive days and has been hugely popular as a rock festival since its inception in 1985. The two festivals are held in different locations with 'Rock am Ring' at the Nürburgring race track and 'Rock im Park' at the Zeppelinfeld in Nuremberg, although both festivals are part of the same event with identical line ups over both days. All artists perform one day at Nürburgring and another day in Nuremberg during the three-day event. Combined together this makes Rock im Park and Rock am Ring the largest music festival held in Germany, and one of the largest in the world. It has a combined attendance of over 150,000 people and usually sells out completely. Lenny headlined the event over the two days with 50,000 people attending the first night and 70,000 the second. Also attending this year were Carlos Santana, Neil Young, Muse and

Faithless amongst many more. Two days later on May 20th he performed again at Pinkpop Festival in the Netherlands with an attendance of 63,000 people. Again Muse were on the listing alongside Lenny, heading across from Rock am Ring.

Moving on to to Denmark Lenny's set list had evolved slightly and followed, roughly, the following format: 'Bank Robber Man', 'Rock and Roll Is Dead', 'Is There Any Love in Your Heart', 'Dig In', 'Pay to Play', 'Beyond the 7th Sky', 'Let Love Rule', 'More Than Anything in This World', 'Stillness of Heart', 'Blues for Sister Someone', 'If I Could Fall in Love' and 'Fields of Joy'. 'Are You Gonna Go My Way' and 'Mama Said' were also added to the setlist. After a concert in Sweden Lenny returned to Germany once again for his own stand-alone concerts in Hanover and Berlin.

After two shows in Spain at Madrid and Barcelona Lenny and his band played two further festivals in Italy, starting with Cornetto Free in Rome. The Gelato company had sponsored the huge event which was also tied up with auditions to find new bands and other activities. The festival, held in June, was located at three sites; as well as Rome where Lenny performed there were additional concerts at Piazza Duomo in Milan and Piazza del Popolo in Naples. The second festival Lenny played in Italy was the Festivalbar held at Verona, where Lenny played a similar set to the Rock am Ring and Cornetto Free events. Throughout June Lenny played concerts in Switzerland, again in Germany and then in Austria before he returned to England for a concert at Wembley Arena on June 17th. He played a smaller, more intimate set at The Astoria a day later on the 18th. He finished the European leg with two shows in France before returning to the US where he played through July, making his way up to Canada. Lenny's concert reviews were nothing short of brilliant; with six albums under his belt and the greatest hits collection the crowds in their thousands were now full Kravitz fans and every song he performed was met with wild pandemonium as he blasted through his songs, new and old.

Lenny was now being supported by Pink, who had reportedly sent Lenny some custom-made Pink Underwear that had 'The Pink Lenny Tour 2002' written on them, with the hope of joining him as he made his way around the arenas of the US and Canada; it worked, and she supported him in Vancouver on 24th August 2002.

Alecia Beth Moore or Pink, or P!nk, was originally a member of the girl group Choice. In 1995 LaFace Records saw Choice and wanted Pink as a solo act, so she signed with them and her first album *Can't Take Me Home* was released in 2000; it was a great success and went double platinum in the US. It also had two hits on the Billboard Hot 100, 'There You Go' and 'Most Girls'. Shortly after she found further success with the collaborative single 'Lady Marmalade' which was taken from the *Moulin Rouge* soundtrack; the cover was a hit worldwide increasing her popularity. She released her second album *Missundaztood* a year later in 2001 and it went on to sell more than 13 million copies worldwide. It had three monster hits associated with it which hit the number one spot worldwide: 'Get the Party Started', 'Don't Let Me Get Me', and 'Just Like a Pill'.

The Vancouver concert was typical of Lenny's shows around this tour: Pink would kick it off with 'Get the Party Started' and for many of Lenny's fans this would have been the first time they would have had the chance to see her live, although she did now have a significant following of her own and her own fans also attended the shows. Her set also included 'Don't Let Me Get Me', 'There You Go', 'M!ssundaztood' and her latest single recently released 'Just Like A Pill'. She also frequently paid tribute to the late Janis Joplin and sang a couple of her tracks. Lenny himself came on in silhouette, working the entrance as the major star he now was, dressed in tight waisted bellbottoms with his pristine Afro and trademark guitar. Lenny was now the full-on rock star working the show through his stadium made songs both new and old, working his set list to perfection and giving the crowd exactly what they wanted. The new album *Lenny* was perfect in sound to transform its contents into great live performances. The show started typically with 'Battlefield of Love' before moving through to new tracks such as 'If I Could Fall in Love' and 'Stillness of Heart'. Lenny also had a habit of venturing offstage into the crowd, giving the security teams a hard time in following him as he disappeared in a frenzy of hands and the crowd swallowed him whole. There was also the now infamous drum solo by Cindy Blackford which gave Lenny time to pop backstage and change; the solo was a huge highlight and with her massive Afro it was a fantastic musical spectacle for the delighted crowd. The second half of the show kept the hits and crowd favourites at the fore as Lenny and his band blasted through 'Rock and Roll is Dead', Let Love Rule' and 'Are You Gonna Go My Way'; he would then play 'Again' and the re-energised rock anthem 'American Woman'. After thanking the crowd with the usual goodnight, Lenny would return with 'Fly Away' as the final encore. It was a show that now had the perfect timing and longevity; Lenny was at the stage in his career where he had enough new material to showcase perfectly and slot in with his ever-increasing back catalogue of stadium-friendly tunes.

Continuing with the tour Lenny performed concerts in September at Las Vegas at Mandalay Bay Events Centre, California, Phoenix, and Mexico where he played at Estadio Azteco in Mexico City, where he concluded his tour on 7th September 2002. Lenny next appeared in a special show of *The Simpsons*, in a show entitled 'How I Spent my Summer Vacation'; the show was the second episode of *The Simpsons'* fourteenth season and was eventually aired a couple of months later on November 10 on the Fox Network. This episode was promoted more than most mainly due to the large list of high-profile stars, which included Lenny. The title of the episode was a play on words, referencing Joe Strummer of The Clash; in something of an unfortunate coincidence, it featured many stars in the episode including Mick Jagger, Keith Richards, Elvis Costello and Tom Petty. Personally, Lenny was now dating Brazilian model Adriana Lima and earlier this year the pair got engaged, although the relationship would be short lived and soon after the engagement was called off.

Lenny contributed to another album when, on November 12th 2002, rapper Jay Z released his album *The Blueprint 2: The Gift & the Curse*, which was later styled as *The Blueprint²: The Gift & the Curse*. It would be his seventh studio album and was released by Roc-A-Fella Records and Def Jam Recordings. The album serves as a follow on to his sixth album *The Blueprint* which was released a year earlier. Different parts of the album were later taken and reissued, and they featured on a compilation album, titled *Blueprint 2.1.* which was released a year later in 2003. There were many artists and rappers who appeared and contributed to the album; these were, amongst others, Dr Dre, Beyoncé, Timbaland, Jimmy Kendrick and many more. Lenny contributed to the track 'Guns & Roses', and the album debuted at number one in the US.

With the album *Lenny*, and the tour that followed, he had once again maintained the status of a truly global rock star: his incredible live shows, flanked by his established and solid band members, kept the fans flocking to see him in their hundreds of thousands around the world. He was also now well established on the worldwide festival circuit benefitting from his chart hits and consistent catchy well-written rock tunes. Lenny was now in addition looking at other avenues to pursue. He was looking into interior design, which was something he was extremely passionate about; also he was moving slowly into other media projects and making small cameo appearances in various films. Over the past couple of years Lenny Kravitz had once again risen to the top and sustained himself as a true rock star, with an incredible ability to recreate his influences in a truly unique way. He was indeed *The Minister of Rock 'n' Roll...*

Photo © Laurent Valay

Baptised in the Electric Church

In March 2003 America launched the first phase of its invasion of Iraq. There was a well-publicised build up to the invasion and it lasted for around a month; the USA was joined by the UK, Australia and Poland and it caused widespread protests within the countries involved. Lots of key figures vented their opinions on the invasion, which many thought was a reaction to 9/11 with the US looking to end the so called 'War on Terror'. What many in the US were worried about was a repeat of Vietnam and for those key figures and artists this got the creativity flowing through their various channels. TV was debating it, politicians were debating it, radio was debating it and all over the world the invasion was reported and watched closely. Lenny held his own musical protest against the invasion when he released the track 'We Want Peace'. This was available as a download-only track which he performed alongside singer Kadim Al-Saher who was well established as one of the most successful singers in the Arab world, himself from Iraq.

They released the track through the Rock the Vote platform, which is a non-profit organisation that holds itself on the slogan 'to engage and build the political power of young people'. The group was originally founded in 1990 by Virgin Records America co-chairman Jeff Ayeroff and the platform had a clear direction, being set up to get young people involved in politics and to encourage them to vote; as a result unsurprisingly it had increasing voter turnout among the 18-24 age group. The organisation is known for its strength 'through celebrity' and has a partnership through MTV. Many celebrities and high-profile stars had been involved with Rock the Vote including Madonna, The Red Hot Chili Peppers, Leonardo DiCaprio, Justin Timberlake,

Samuel Jackson and many more. Lenny's song with Kadim Al-Saher reached number 1 on the world internet download charts and also on the MP3.com download chart.

On March 23rd the second album by N.E.R.D was released, *Fly or Die*. It became a huge worldwide album and featured Lenny on one of the tracks, the single 'Maybe', the song also featuring Questlove on drums. The song was initially only released in the UK, where it reached number 25, and a year later it was released in the US. The track was used on an iPod commercial which also promoted the song. The track used a sample from Lupe Fiasco, the song 'And He Gets the Girl', which was a non-album track released alongside the single 'I Gotcha' which was from Lupe Fiasco's *Food & Liquor*.

Lenny now started to formulate his next offering and spent time at Hotel Edison Studios in Miami recording songs that would appear on his next album, *Baptism*, his seventh studio album. He also started to venture into other areas that he was particularly interested in, especially interior design. He set up and founded Kravitz Design Inc. which based itself in New York; it primarily concentrated on commercial and residential designs and started to work with various clients. The client list they worked with included the Morgans Hotel Group, Swarovski Crystal, and The Setai Group. Later the company would expand further and collaborate with Flavor Paper wallpaper working on its Tropicalismo collection inspired by Brazil's tropicalia art movement from the 1960s. More success for Kravitz Design followed when Swarovski selected Kravitz Design Inc. in 2005 and 2006 to participate in their Crystal Palace Collection. The company also worked on a luxury recording studio for The Setai Resort and Residences in Miami Beach, New York, Paris and New Orleans. The company gave Lenny a focus outside of music and within an area he was particularly interested in, that of luxury interior design; that said, the music didn't stop and Lenny stayed within the studio crafting his next album which he worked through during 2003.

A month before the release date of *Baptism* he put out the first single from the album, 'Why Are We Runnin?' on April 10th 2004. The single was written again in collaboration with Craig Ross with the production done by Lenny, and as before with previous singles it benefitted from some cross media; this time it became a playable song on the video game Guitar Hero on Tour: Modern Hits and it was also used in the opening credits for the TV series *Heldt* which was popular in Germany at the time. The single came with two B-sides, 'Uncharted Terrain' and 'Destiny'; the US version just had 'Uncharted Terrain' as an additional track. Lenny said at the time that the song was inspired by the lives of modern-day rock stars and if the video was anything to go by then this made perfect sense as it followed this narrative. The video was directed by French/American photographer and video director Philip Andelman who would go on to work with Lenny on music videos in the future. It showcases a life of complete excess and starts with Lenny and a host of women waking up in a hotel room surrounded by empty drinks bottles and drugs. On leaving the hotel through screaming fans they board a private jet where the hedonism continues before they arrive at the next concert and perform. Lenny is seen at the end looking worse for wear and slumped on a chair after a concert. The message is clear from how Lenny first described the inspiration for the song and it acted out as such, showing the dangerous side to rock and roll and the excess some participate in when touring. The single didn't perform as well as expected and hovered around the edge of the charts in most countries.

Baptism was released on May 18th 2004, again on Virgin records, and was originally a project Lenny pursued in a different direction from what was eventually released: Lenny intended it to be a pure 1970s funk album, and in fact it was intended to be called just that, *The Funk Album*. Somewhere near the end of the recording sessions Lenny had a change of heart and added some acoustic guitar songs and the album changed somewhat, so he then renamed it. It then followed the path of a more standard rock album with a mixture of Kravitz type tunes as opposed to a pure album of funk driven songs. The album features rapper Jay Z who Lenny had recently worked with on Jay Z's own album, *The Blueprint²: The Gift & the Curse*; he featured on the track 'Storm'. Lenny also revived the cancelled track he originally worked with alongside Michael Jackson, '(I Can't Make It) Another Day'. The decision Lenny made to change the album from its original idea wasn't met with favourably by his record label. Lenny was at the time going through personal problems and suffering from depression, which had led the label to question some of the darker material that appeared on the reworked *Baptism*. The album does focus on Lenny's mindset, and there are many hints within the lyrics throughout; the title track itself has a message of epiphany and the cover has Lenny submerged in a giant pool of blood, or paint, and naked apart from a guitar. There is also of course the first single which, along with the video, questions the excess lifestyle involved in rock and roll which Lenny was observing, or partaking in. It's an album where he may be looking for acceptance, spirituality or something more meaningful.

It's here where we pause for thought. Albums like this are often criticised by a record company because the album itself changed direction during the writing and recording process. Many albums in the past have changed course through the recording as new songs take hold or situations change; the record company will then be surprised when an album is presented to them that has drastically changed from the one that they were initially expecting. A true artist like Lenny Kravitz would always be steered by that process: he would have been guided by the music, and not the other way around. The original album that was planned may well have been more commercially successful but the very fact that Lenny let the artistic direction change, even if it was into something more downbeat and darker in its feel, should be to his credit. If he, as a musician, writer and performer, was feeling depressed and questioning the industry he was in, then this would and should pour into his songs - and this is what happened, and the record company didn't like it. Lenny let it happen and *Baptism* was a true album, not a commercially seeking one.

The lyrics show an insight into Lenny's thoughts and emotions during this period and it's this that again stands out head and shoulders above the increasing sludge of manufactured pop bands churning out the same systematic drizzle from the pop production line. *Baptism* is Lenny taking control once more: the majority of the album is him - he plays most of the basics throughout: drums, guitars, percussion - again showcasing his musical abilities. There were others who naturally contributed and they are listed as personnel: David Baron on saxophone, Henry Hirsch on piano, bass guitar and some drums, David Sanborn on tenor saxophone, Craig Ross on guitars and some piano and no less than seven people named for hand clapping; all other instruments are from Lenny. The production however is what the critical focus seemed to be on. Piano and strings for example are buried amongst high drums and low sounding guitars, and again he gets accused of 'borrowing' heavily from others: 'All Along The Watchtower' one example of many on 'I Don't Want To Be a Star', and of course there was the continuous Prince comparison when he presented anything remotely funky, namely in this instance 'Sistamamlover'.

Lenny started his tour in promotion of the album with an appearance again at Pinkpop Festival 2004 before heading over to Europe. He played first in Denmark before moving across to Germany and France. The setlist for the new tour roughly ran with the following: 'Why Are We Runnin?', 'Always on The Run', 'It Ain't Over 'Till it's Over', 'Again', 'California', 'Fields of Joy', 'Dig In', 'Fear', 'American Woman', 'Fly Away', 'Are You Gonna Go My Way', 'I Belong to You'. After France Lenny played again at Super Bock Super Rock in Portugal, the festival this year running from the 9th through to the 11th July, and Lenny played his set on the last day; it was attended by around 35,000 fans at Palco Principal. On the first day of the festival on June 9th Lenny released the second single from *Baptism*, 'California'. The track is a great symbol of an autobiographical song with Lenny reflecting back to his move to California from New York. It has a good vibe and there is a summer feel to the track, and the music fits the feel of the lyrics. The music video is slightly amateurish and not to the quality of Lenny's past videos; it feels very in-house and shows the band on stage intertwined with scenes of kids messing around on skateboards and on the surf. He played concerts in Spain and the Netherlands in mid-June before attending Heineken Jammin Festival on 20th June in Milan. The festival had been around for six years since its inception in mid-June 1998 at the Imola Autodrome and had a huge attendance; over the three-day event it would attract over 100,000 fans. A few years forward from now, on the tenth anniversary of the festival, the location was moved to Mestre, Parco San Giuliano. Lenny headed to Belgium next for a concert at Rock Werchter 2004, another huge festival attracting around 65,000 fans annually. Headlining the three-day event this year were Metallica, Basement Jaxx and Lenny on day three, and many other acts played over the three days including The Cure, Pink, Muse, Moloko, Placebo and PJ Harvey. Next came England, where Lenny's popularity was always incredibly strong; he played at Wembley Arena on July 7th, the NEC Birmingham on July 10th and then Party in The Park located in Hyde Park London. The name Party in The Park is generic and is the name given as it's organised by different organisations and media outlets in the UK, mainly radio stations and other groups. It's held throughout the summer and as the name suggests is located in various large parks with a focus on being a family-friendly event. On the list in 2004 were Alanis Morissette, Lionel Richie, The Corrs and many others including Lenny, although the listing was mainly low-level acts with little quality apart from Alanis, Lionel and Lenny himself. In July Lenny and the band travelled to Japan for three shows before he headed for the US leg of his tour.

On August 14th Lenny released the third single from *Baptism*, the song 'Storm' featuring Jay Z. The video shows Lenny walking down the street and interacting with various people; again, as with the video for 'California', it feels very in-house and low budget. Lenny also has a new look: his hair had changed once more, the long locks had gone and he was sporting a shorter look but still wearing his trademark bellbottom jeans and shades. Jay Z does not appear on the video and during his rap, which is the standard tired format of the rapper coming in for a few choice verses two thirds through, his vocals are lip synced by Lenny himself.

In September Lenny started rocking the States, starting in Maine before a concert at Borgato Events Centre in Atlanta. In October the fourth scheduled single was released, 'Calling All Angels'. The video shows Lenny sitting at the piano in an empty room composing the song; he is bare footed and the video is shot in black and white. The video also shows Lenny playing a small drum kit in the room and is interspersed with shots of a woman walking around a cemetery. The video is a reflection of grief, loss and loneliness and is a great example of how the original album was changed to accommodate what Lenny wanted to achieve on the album. Lenny attended the MTV Video Music Awards and then The American Music Awards a month later in November, and he also released the final single from the album, 'Lady', on November 23rd - and it became a surprising hit. The single was rumoured to have been written about his girlfriend at the time, the actress Nicole Kidman. Again, cross media made the single stand out as it was used heavily in advertisements for GAP. The commercials show Lenny dancing and singing to Sarah Jessica Parker and brought a great deal of attention to the song. The intro to the commercial features the opening riff to 'Are You Gonna Go My Way' before going back into the chords of 'Lady'. On the commercials Lenny is featured with his long hair, but by the time the video for the song was shot, he had his shorter clipped version. The B-side, or additional track, was a remix of 'Storm' previously released as 'Just Blaze Remix'. 'Lady' reached number 27 on the Billboard Hot 100, making it a surprising hit, especially considering it was the final single from the album; however it was certainly helped with the ongoing exposure from the adverts. The video was again directed by Philip Andelman and it shows Lenny playing guitar and singing on a circular stage with women dancing around him, naturally. The lighting around him changes throughout as the sound intensifies through the song. Compared to 'Calling All Angels' it has a completely different feel, and is more of a celebration and performance than anything that holds a deeper message, and this fits in with the song itself.

Lenny kicked off 2005 by heading with the band to Mexico and Chile for concerts through March, starting in Monterrey at the Coca-Cola Auditorio. Continuing in South America he played in Chile at Estadio Nacional in Santiago before heading to Argentina where he played on 11th and 12th March at the home of Boca Juniors in Buenos Aires, concluding the South American leg of the tour with concerts in Brazil before heading back and performing through Texas. The South American tour became a symbolic one and also a historic one. Lenny had achieved the largest tour by an international artist ever. It culminated with a full-blown rocking performance in front of over 300,000 fans at the 440th anniversary party of Rio de Janeiro at Copacabana Beach - the largest international free concert ever produced. He would return in a few years alongside The Rolling Stones but for now it was Lenny Kravitz on Copacabana Beach and over 300,000 fans.

Again, as always, the reviews of Lenny's concerts were excellent and he ripped through the sets night after night. He had changed the set list again slightly during the tour with the set now following the format of 'Minister of Rock and Roll', 'Live', 'Let Love Rule', 'It Ain't Over Till It's Over', 'Why are We Running?', 'Is There Any Love In Your Heart', 'American Woman', 'Tunnel Vision', 'Be', 'Stand By My Woman', 'Always on the Run' and 'Are You Gonna Go My Way?'

Lenny and the band made their way through the US for a 27-date tour playing mainly theatres, something Lenny was looking forward to as he hadn't played them for a while. Travelling north through April and May, he played 13 concerts throughout May alone in 2005 and all to incredible reviews. After the US leg of the tour Lenny headed to Europe starting in Italy on June 3rd; he played three shows in Italy at Verona, Florence and Assago at the Filaforum. Three shows in Spain followed before Lenny played another festival, this time The Algarve Summer Festival in Portugal, which is held annually at Stadium Algarve in Faro. Because of the incredible demand Lenny returned to Spain for an additional three concerts before heading to France, starting at Le Grand Rex in Paris, which is the largest cinema theatre in Europe and known for its stunning decoration; the venue also hosts the annual Jules Verne Adventure Film Festival each April, a six-day event which attracts more than 48,000 attendees. On June 25th and 26th Lenny played two more festivals: the first was the TW Classic Festival which is held in Werchter, Belgium annually as a one-day event, and the next night Lenny played at Rockin Park 2005.

Lenny played the very first Rockin Park festival on 26th June 2005, which was held at the Goffertpark in Nijmegen in the Netherlands and was set up to honour the 2000th anniversary of the city. It was originally organised by Mojo Concerts and had over 35,000 people attending the first edition of the festival. Later in June 2008 the second edition of Rockin Park took place, again in the Goffertpark in Nijmegen, and this year the event again attracted a significant amount of people, around 30,000 visitors; this event was also partly broadcast directly by radio channel 3FM. Year three was equally successful with Pearl Jam headlining, but year four, held in 2012, which was headlined by Snow Patrol, was a disappointment. The 2012 festival, with Snow Patrol as the headline, struggled with disappointing ticket sales and since this the event was not repeated, the organisers switching their attention from here on to organising a multi-day festival, and so the Rockin Park was no more. Lenny played the first and largest and again gave an incredible show for the 35,000 fans crammed in to rock with him.

Lenny continued north and played in Oslo, at The Oslo Spektrum, before heading to Stockholm and then to Finland, playing at the 13,000 capacity Hartwall Arena in Helsinki before heading across to Russia for a concert at St Petersburg at Ledovy Dvorets. On the 15th June Lenny played at the Moon and Stars event which takes place annually in Locarno, Switzerland, typically at the beginning of July. Over the seven-day event a different headline would feature every night. The event was founded in 2004 through a collaboration with Good News Production AG and over the years it had gained a significant following; in fact the festival attracts around 85,000-90,000 visitors over the course of the event. Headlining in 2005 were Seal, supported by Chris Piece; Jamiroquai, supported by James Blunt; Coldplay, supported by Richard Ashcroft; Laura Pausini, supported by Le Vibrazioni; Joe Cocker, supported by Katie Melua; and Lenny closing the last day, supported by Nikka Costa. Lenny played to an estimated 53,000 fans.

Three days later on 19th July Lenny played at The Paléo Festival de Nyon, which is usually just shortened to Paléo. Again held annually the festival is held in Switzerland in Nyon about 25 miles east of Geneva. Paleo initially started way back in 1976 as a small Folk Festival for the people of Nyon but had grown substantially since. It grew to become one of the major open-air music festivals in mainland Europe, and became the biggest in Switzerland, and lasts for six days through July, typically Tuesday through to Sunday. On the final day after the headline act there is usually a huge fireworks display with music. When Lenny played in 2005, 3.5 million spectators and 2500 artists had been part of the Paléo Festival to date.

Lenny returned to the UK to bring his tour to a conclusion at the end of July. He played at Hammersmith Apollo on July 21st before the final concert of The Electric Church Tour at Carling Academy in Brixton on July 22nd. The tour had been an incredible success. Even though *Baptism* was originally intended to be something different, *The Funk Album*, Lenny had followed his artistic vision on how the album should be and the content within it. It had a poor start but with Lenny's constant touring and the singles that followed his popularity was once again established as a truly worldwide star with an enviable back catalogue of hits and songs to carry any festival or concert. The tour was a sell out, with Lenny having to return to some countries just to meet demand, and he had made history in South America, playing at one concert alone to over 300,000 fans. It would be four years until his next album but this would not stop Lenny touring. Lenny had been baptised well and truly in the electric church, and he now joined an entourage to tour further; but not just your average entourage, one of rock royalty - what a show this will be - it's not so much 'Why Are We Running?' more *'Walk This Way'*...

Photo © Laurent Valay

Lenny, Rockin' the Joint

In August 2005 Hurricane Katrina hit New Orleans, devastating the city. Katrina was one of the most destructive tropical cyclones and one of the costliest natural disasters in the history of the US; it was also one of deadliest - over 1,245 people died in the hurricane and the subsequent floods that followed giving it the highest death count since 1928. The damage was also huge, estimated to be a staggering $108 billion.

Hitting the city on August 29th 2005, the destruction of New Orleans began when over fifty breaches, which were supposed to be in place to protect the city, failed, and it was this which resulted in the majority of the deaths. It led to around 80% of the entire city becoming completely flooded, and the floodwater remained for many weeks. There was widespread anger after the disaster and in particular at the response by the authorities. Many felt that because New Orleans was in the South of the country it was left almost abandoned at the time. The images of the people of New Orleans, and the resulting devastation, were shown for weeks in the US and indeed all around the world. As a result, a benefit concert was set up to aid in the relief effort and Lenny was involved. He performed in New York at the simulcast which was broadcast alongside the main concert in aid of the disaster at the New York studios of NBC. The benefit concert itself was held to raise awareness and money for the cause. A Concert for Hurricane Relief was held on September 2nd 2005 and during the event viewers were encouraged to donate to the American Red Cross Disaster Relief Fund by calling a number, or through the Red Cross's website. The benefit generated $50 million and was watched on television by approximately 8.5 million viewers.

In October 2005 rock band Aerosmith released a live album entitled *Rockin' the Joint*. The album was recorded in January 2002 at The Joint at the Hard Rock Hotel in Las Vegas, and consists of Aerosmith classics mixed in with more recent songs performed live. The band planned the tour that followed the release and as Lenny had always been friends with Aerosmith, he was invited to tour alongside them. The tour was scheduled to run through North America at the end of 2005 and into 2006. The first leg ran from October 30th to February 24th and all these shows were opened by Lenny and his band. The second leg was scheduled to run from March to April 2006; these shows were smaller by comparison and were opened this time by veteran rock band Cheap Trick. The tour wasn't without its issues as lead singer Steven Tyler required throat surgery so it was disrupted throughout.

On October 29th 2005 Lenny was told his father had died after a short fight with leukaemia; the next night, on October 30th, when Lenny was scheduled to perform ahead of Aerosmith, he announced the news to the crowd, and he dedicated 'Let Love Rule' to his father during the performance. Steven Tyler managed to perform through his throat issues but widespread reports were circulating around about this as concerts were shorter than expected for fans, the initial set list had dropped and many fans were venting frustration at the relatively short sets when they paid a high price for tickets. The ticket prices themselves were as high as $150 and even the cheaper seats were in excess of $85. The setlist issue was another area often criticised: the setlist the band played initially started at around 20 songs but this was noticeably reduced to around 16 songs and it was evident this was done to sustain the tour to completion; sadly though this didn't happen for the band and it left many fans feeling that they were not getting their money's worth out of the concerts. An announcement was made on March 22nd 2006 that Steven Tyler needed throat surgery and thus the remaining dates of the tour were cancelled. Additionally, the band themselves was put on hiatus indefinitely until Steven Tyler fully recovered. Lenny himself also had some reported issues when before the Tampa Florida show he didn't perform, which was explained as being due to some voice complications. The band employed a unique stage setup which featured two long catwalks, extending slightly diagonally from the main stage. This allowed the band, and Lenny when he was opening, to have more flexibility in working the crowd, and giving all seats a better view of the band members while they were performing. Despite the shorter sets the tour was a huge success both financially and for the reputation of Aerosmith and Lenny. As well as the live album Aerosmith also released a DVD that had four tracks on it from the shows.

In January 2006 Lenny released a song through absolutracks which was a series of promotional tracks for Absolut Vodka. It was available as an mp3 from absoluttracks.com. The track Lenny submitted was remixed by ten musical producers and distributed online.

In May 2006 Madonna launched her Confessions Tour in support of her tenth studio album, *Confessions on a Dance Floor*. The concert was widely reported on, as with all Madonna concerts, and it was very visual and theme orientated. It was divided into four parts, those being Equestrian, Bedouin, Glam-Punk, and Disco. The Equestrian section had horse-themed, bondage performances, the Bedouin had performances accompanied by various statements and messages, the Glam-Punk performances had Madonna playing guitars and the final Disco segment consisted of dancing in general. The tour was critically applauded for its presentation and it was extremely commercially successful, as all venues sold out within hours of announcement; in fact the demand was so high additional dates needed to be added. The tour had the status of becoming the highest-grossing tour ever for a female artist: it achieved over $194.7 million from 60 shows, and had 1.2 million spectators. It also gained the highest-grossing music tour per concert record in the 2007 edition of the *Guinness World Records*. The Confessions Tour received the Most Creative Stage Production award at the Pollstar Concert Industry Awards as well as Top Boxscore from the Billboard Touring Awards. During many of the shows as it toured Lenny was seen attending in the crowd, and he eventually joined Madonna live on stage to play guitar on the song 'I Love New York' at the last of four shows in Paris.

Adding to his design company Lenny founded a design firm which he named Kravitz Design. He loved the creative side of design and even stated that if he hadn't been a musician, he would have been a designer. The new venture would focus on interior and furniture design. It went on to design residential spaces, as well as a chandelier for the crystal company Swarovski which was named 'Casino Royale.'

On Christmas Day 2006 another legendary name, and one of the most influential musicians of all time, died. It was a name connected to many modern artists who ventured their sound into funk territory, and this was an area synonymous with Lenny's work. James Brown died from congestive heart failure resulting from complications of pneumonia. He was 73 years old. After Brown's death a host of celebrities along with thousands of fans gathered for a public memorial service at the Apollo Theatre in New York City on December 28th. The Godfather of Soul was without doubt a key influence within 20th century music, and many artists, including Lenny, were connected to Brown's sound in some way; in fact James Brown was so influential that you only had to play anything remotely funky within your music, or lyrically replicate him in any way, to be compared. No-one however could say that James Brown was like anyone else - he was unique, a pure invention of himself, and his legacy touched anyone who was writing songs that had any funk within them, Lenny included.

Moving into 2007 Lenny next appeared at the Rock for the Rainforest 2007 event held on May 19th. The concerts started out as annually but were now held biennially. The concert was held, as the name suggests, by the Rainforest Foundation Fund and Rainforest Foundation US and is hosted by the organisation's founders Sting and his wife Trudie Styler, since 1991. As a result, and as expected, Sting holds regular performances, and these also include regular performances from the likes of Elton John, Billy Joel and James Taylor. The event holds the Guinness World Record for the largest environmental fundraising event; in fact by 1996 the concerts had raised over $6,000,000, by 2000, more than $11,000,000 and by 2004 it had raised more than $20,000,000. The money raised comes mainly from its corporate sponsorships, individual and group ticket sales, and related events such as silent auctions. At this year's event, which featured Lenny, the Empire State Building was illuminated green on the night of the concert. Funds raised by the concerts and events go towards the projects that benefit the indigenous peoples of the world's rainforests. The Rainforest Foundation Fund supports these projects by three independent national organisations: Rainforest Foundation Norway, Rainforest Foundation US, and Rainforest Foundation UK. The concert in 2006 included performances by Sting, Billy Joel, Sheryl Crow and Lenny, and it raised over $2.3 million for the cause.

Next Lenny gave his talents to another cause when in June he released a version of the track 'Cold Turkey', originally written by John Lennon, which was for the charity CD *Instant Karma*. The CD was in aid of The Amnesty International Campaign to Save Darfur. The compilation album consisted of various artists covering songs by John Lennon to benefit Amnesty International's campaign to alleviate the crisis in Darfur. The album and campaign were part of a bigger initiative which was Amnesty International's global Make Some Noise project. Yoko Ono permitted the rights to Lennon's songs and music publishing royalties and they were donated to Amnesty. Contributing to the album as well as Lenny were U2, R.E.M, Corrine Bailey Rae, Aerosmith and Christina Aguilera amongst others. The US had two CD versions released; the primary version was a two-disc set containing 23 tracks with the second having a two-disc set sold only at Borders retail outlets but this was essentially the same apart from a bonus track. On iTunes there was an expanded digital release available in the US that added 11 further tracks to the 23 tracks on the primary CD release, making it a 34-track digital set.

Lenny now started putting together tracks and formulating them into an album that he planned to release in 2008. Before then though he continued with his charity work and performances in aid of various charitable causes. Next was a huge one when, on July 7th 2007, he performed again at Copacabana beach at the Brazilian leg of Live Earth in Rio de Janeiro. His appearance made him one of only three major international rock stars to perform two huge free concerts at the world-famous beach venue, along with Macy Gray and the Rolling Stones. Previously Lenny had brought in around 300,000 fans, and this time he managed to add another 100,000 to that. This Earth Tour event had eight other acts on the bill alongside Lenny, and they performed in front of 400,000 people at the beach.

In September Lenny contributed to a Fats Domino tribute album called *Goin' Home; A Tribute to Fats Domino*. Lenny played on the track 'Whole Lotta Lovin' along with Troy 'Trombone' Shorty Andrews, Fred Wesley, Pee Wee Ellis and legendary saxophonist Maceo Parker who was at the time touring with Prince.

Towards the end of 2007 Lenny played at a few venues in between finalising his next album. He performed at Cow Palace in California as well a performance at The American Music Awards in November where he performed 'I'll Be Waiting'. Lenny also appeared at the Grey Cup halftime show in Toronto at the Rogers Centre on November 25 where the American Football team the Saskatchewan Roughriders beat the Winnipeg Blue Bombers. Also, Lenny filmed the video for 'I'll Be Waiting' in Central Park in New York City, directed by Marc Webb, although this version was later shelved to be replaced by a new version, with Lenny co-directing alongside Philip Andelman; this version was filmed in Lenny's New York City recording studio. The video would premier later on VH1's Top 20 Countdown in January 2008.

In December Lenny and the band played a show at Sacramento in California but before the year was out, and with his new album completed, Lenny released the first single from the now named *It Is Time For A Love Revolution*. 'I'll Be Waiting' was released on December 6th and was accompanied by the new version of the video filmed within Lenny's studio. Again the song is written with Craig Ross. Although 'I'll Be Waiting' was scheduled as the first single the track 'Bring It On' had been previously released but this was only as a radio-only single to US rock stations. The iTunes download release date for the song was November 6, 2007. 'I'll Be Waiting' is another power ballad sitting within Lenny's genre; the track is familiar to a lot of Lenny's previous tunes within this field starting with a simple piano chord and then the guitar riff over the top as the chorus comes in. Lyrically Lenny sings of waiting for someone and is heartbroken

106

from a past relationship, and he realises she is the one he really loved. The single was a great success, especially across Europe, where it went to the top of various charts in Czech Republic, Italy, the Netherlands, Belgium, and Switzerland. In Germany the single reached the top 10 making it his most successful single to date, as well as in Austria and Slovakia. It was less successful in the US, reaching the mid-70s on the Billboard Hot 100. The new accompanying video was also a success. It shows Lenny working in the studio and is shot in black and white. It showcases Lenny's recording process and is more a demonstration of his multi-instrumentalism than offering any sort of story within the video: he is shown playing the piano, the drums, the guitar, and the bass, and simply singing the song throughout the video. He is also shown towards the end directing the orchestra on the track for the bridge, which is a superb highlight to the song as Lenny once again shows his musical ability, just in case anyone was in doubt as to who was pulling the strings.

As well as the performance at the American Music Awards Lenny saw the new year in with a performance of the track on the 2008 *Dick Clark's New Year's Rockin' Eve Show*, the annual New Year's Eve special showcased live from New York City's Times Square. It shows the annual ball drop event, along with live and pre-recorded musical performances by popular musicians from Times Square and Hollywood. It also shows live performances from festivals from New Orleans. 'I'll Be Waiting' was also featured in the end credits to the film *L: Change the World* released in 2008, a Japanese film which was a spin-off to the Death Note film series.

In the past couple of years Lenny had showed his charitable side; he had appeared in front of 300,000 people and this year had broken his own record and performed in front of 400,000. He had also supported Aerosmith and many other charitable and worthy causes through his releases and performances. Now as we enter 2008 his new single was high in the charts and airplay systems around the world and his new album was ready to be released. It was time now for Lenny to tour again, and on his own terms. He started planning the concerts and immediately they started to sell out: the demand was incredible, his fans were waiting once again to rock with Lenny around the world, and ready for *'Dancin... 'til Dawn'*...

Photo © Romain Pasquini

Photo © Laurent Valay

Revolution

With the first single from his new album, 'I'll Be Waiting', still performing well in the various chart systems all over the world, Lenny released his eighth studio album *It Is Time for a Love Revolution*. It would be his last album with Virgin records and was officially released on February 5th 2008. The 14 tracks have the now familiar attributed line - composed, arranged, performed, and produced by Lenny Kravitz - showcasing another one-man band album with Lenny taking full control of events; that said, he had his usual contributors in the studio. Lenny played acoustic guitar, electric guitar, harmonica, piano, electric piano, harpsichord, Hammond B-3 organ, Wurlitzer organ, Mellotron, keyboards, synthesiser, Moog synthesiser, bass, drums, congas, cowbells, tambourine and hand claps. Just to top the listing off he even gave himself credits for sound effects. Again as always Craig Ross adds in acoustic guitar and electric guitar and Liuh-Wen Ting gets a credit for the viola. Critically *It Is Time for a Love Revolution* gained Lenny his strongest reviews for years and what was interesting was the very thing that Lenny had been criticised for in the past, that being borrowing too much from his list of influences, was now starting to be applauded. The album title was Lenny reaffirming the stance he had from his first album, *Let Love Rule* - it's a mantra he had always held strong since the writing on the wall, and it's a phrase he stayed true to and used extensively as a positive message; this was Lenny taking it a step further. Love was always a central theme in his albums, whether person to person, social, or in any other connotation, and Lenny now wanted to take the message more hardcore. He commented at the time that he felt the world was such a negative place at times, with war in every corner. He felt that people were dying needlessly everywhere and there was no understanding between people and countries. He felt it was time to really get people to join together through his music and in the name of love.

The album raced straight into the Billboard 200 landing at number 4 in the US with sales hitting around the 73,000 copies mark within its first week. This made it Lenny's biggest album since he released his *Greatest Hits* in 2000. The album gained even more progress as Lenny toured and other singles and promotional activity took place. One reoccurring comparison made about the album was to Led Zeppelin, who themselves had a re-emergence in and around 2008; many thought Lenny had tapped into this and launched an album based on Zeppelin. That said, there wasn't an album that Lenny had ever released that didn't somewhere in the mix have Zeppelin described around it; this time though it was thought it was more a tribute to them as opposed to borrowing riffs and arrangements. The title track is another Lenny Kravitz opener in the same vein as 'Are You Gonna Go My Way'; again Zeppelin feels like it has Lenny's attention when he blasts through 'Bring It On', and this follows through the album entirely. Whatever the tapestry of influences, what lies well is the way that Lenny now intertwines the influences together, which makes it seamless and not immediately obvious; it is a patchwork of classic standards all coming together which makes it solely Lenny Kravitz, and it's this that makes it reassuringly familiar but still has the edge in the blend to sound unique. The riff for this song dates back to sessions for the 1993 album *Are You Gonna Go My Way*. On the track 'Will You Marry Me' Lenny initially had a completely different song with a different melody and lyric; he pulled the riff back out and then cut the lyric and the melody. He said at the time that his guitar tech commented the track was depressing - it was about dropping out of society - so challenged Lenny went home that night and wrote completely different lyrics and melodies and put it down.

Other standard comparisons continue to run through the album. The JBs - James Brown's backing band - get a mention in many reviews, as does the album *Dirty Mind* by Prince, a favourite of Lenny when he was at high school. What Lenny has perfected and demonstrated with *It Is Time for a Love Revolution* is creating

111

again an album that feels like a discovery of a past classic, something from the golden age of music, and it's this that Lenny Kravitz does better than anyone. He manages to bridge the gap with an album that feels like something from the past but still stays fresh and current, and that is a very difficult balance to get right. The songs overall have a lot of Jimmy Page type hooks that are powerful in delivery, and the harmonies are also larger than before. There are personal messages within the album that Lenny addresses, one stand out in particular being in connection to his father on 'A Long and Sad Goodbye'. The song is an ode reflecting on the tumultuous relationship Lenny had with his father which was in part due to the cheating on Lenny's beloved mother. Although the pair remained at odds for much of their lives, they made their peace shortly before Sy Kravitz's death from leukaemia in 2005. They reconciled a few weeks before he passed and they spent a lot of time with each other in those last days. Lenny freely admitted that his relationship with his father was strained due to him cheating on his mother and he was basically a mama's boy. Lenny talked openly about an incident that's reflected in the song, a moment when he was in a room with his father on the day he was actually leaving and his mother asked him if he had anything to say to his son before he left; Lenny was expecting his father to say some words of remorse or regret but instead his father said, 'You'll do it too'. Lenny said that he had a lot of demons from moments like that and it affected him deeply, but ultimately, they got over it, and the song therefore is reflecting forgiveness and for Lenny a catharsis.

Lenny also goes back to the Iraq conflict with 'Back in Vietnam', a song clear in its message about Iraq and how Lenny feels it mirrors a lot of the Vietnam crisis, a 'here we are again' type of situation, and on reflection years later he was probably right. The theme is addressed again in the song 'I Want To Go Home', written from the point of view of a soldier; it's Lenny saying I don't care who you are or what side you're on, at some point you will say to yourself I've got to get out of here, I want to go home, and reflecting on how different their lives might have been. Lenny spoke to soldiers about this theme and wrote the song based on what they told him.

This however is a deep as he gets and the rest of the album is within Lenny's strength and depth, that of uncomplicated retro rock indulgence. With 'Love Revolution' Lenny comes closer than ever to his debut, 'Let Love Rule', particularly in its feel and delivery. It's full of vintage riffs and has that hippie feeling throughout, flower powered and funky. It was rumoured at the time that Lenny was practising celibacy in a quest to find a wife and his outlook changed, which channelled into and through the album; it made it sound leaner and he came across as hungrier; it's spiritual and heavy on the standard guitar solos and soothing and mellow through the heartfelt ballads.

The album took time to produce as Lenny was working on his various interior design work and other things in between recording the album. It actually started around the end of 2006. Henry Hirsch started to work on the album for around three weeks before an interval, then Lenny started on other things, before returning to it. This method was the favoured way of working for Lenny and Henry as it gave them some perspective on what went before when they returned to it. The album was recorded the same way as previous albums, although the pair still tried out different sonics to see what sounds they could produce. The method for *It Is Time for a Love Revolution* followed the same path in which Lenny now always worked. He would start the track usually with the drums, and on most of this album it was Lenny on drums with Craig Ross on guitar. Once this was done and they were happy Lenny would add the bass and that was recorded, and it was then onto whatever was next as they built the track. Henry Hirsch confirmed that this typically would be done in around six to eight hours to complete the majority of the recordings, unless there was something in particular they were working on and trying to get the sound for. Lenny, once this was completed, would write the lyrics to the track and then usually come in the next day to record vocals, if he was in New York.

Again, they stayed clear of the industry standard of using Pro Tools and tried to get the right sounds as they went along when recording, mixing instruments as they put them down. If this was done right and they were happy with the mixing it would just be a case of balancing the sound, and this was the preferred method

113

Lenny would work with in the studio for *Love Revolution*. It gave it a rawer sound and it's this that makes it sound retro and vintage at the same time, certainly more satisfying than the standard industry manufactured dross that flooded the charts on the album's release. That said, Lenny and Henry Hirsch did use Pro Tools but not to the detriment to the overall sound they wanted to achieve.

Nearly all of the album was recorded at Edison Studios in Manhattan; the remaining bits and pieces Lenny recorded at his home studios in Miami and France. The studio in New York boasted a 2,500-square-foot live room with an 18-foot ceiling attached to a 500-square-foot control room; the high ceiling was a key note in the studio helping the sound along that they wanted to achieve: it gave it a cleaner sound and was easier to control. The control board in the studio again was key to the sound and not your standard modern day one: they used a 26-input Helios board which was originally manufactured in Britain in the 70s and used for both tracking and mixing. The room's ATC SCM-200 monitors are also British-made with the mic preamps being custom made especially. The sound on *Love Revolution* that stands out clearer than most are the vocals and this is at the centre of the recording; it's this approach that gives Lenny's albums a very distinctive quality and all his albums have this element - it always worked in the past and it worked perfectly here.

The many reviews of the album followed the same path of considering Lenny's influences, and the sound they had, making their way to his own sound. But the use of this equipment was the way Lenny wanted his albums to sound, and it was here that the reviews seem to change and he was accepted for himself; he wasn't blatantly trying to be Led Zeppelin, more wearing his influences on his sleeve, which lie in the 60s and 70s. In essence they made great sounding records and that is at the very core of what Lenny and Henry attempted to reproduce in the studio; the actual melody and construction of the song is all Lenny Kravitz, and no one else. The sound also affects radio because as successful and popular as Lenny was, he still suffered from lack of radio airplay, and still does to this day. The record companies were ever changing and the chart system was constantly moving into other areas. It was a completely different methodology to get airplay than it was 10 or

15 years previously. Only certain acts could gain airplay at key times, and this depended on the label, the station and various other factors. It didn't matter how popular on tour an artist was, if they didn't tick the boxes they were not played, and Lenny was stuck in the middle. Mainly hip hop and black music radio stations for example didn't think he was black enough, and white people and white radio stations didn't think he was white enough, and this continued on as various radio stations catered for certain styles. The same could be said of Prince for example: Lenny and Prince could easily be played on a rock radio station, a funk radio station or even a jazz radio station. Their variety and ingenuity in crossing boundaries through their music made the ever-fragmenting chart, radio and recording contract business too rigid to cope with them, and as a result it was a rare treat to hear someone like Lenny Kravitz played on the radio, and if he was you could probably guess the song, as they would play the same three or four songs every time. One thing that kept true though was the very fact that his fans had been with him and supporting him to this point for over 20 years so in reference to not being played much on the radio it didn't really matter, he was doing something right.

A couple of outside connections made the album have more popularity. The title track was featured on the soundtrack to the film *Made of Honor*, the American romantic comedy which was directed by Paul Weiland and written by Adam Sztykiel, Deborah Kaplan, and Harry Elfont. The film stars Patrick Dempsey, Michelle Monaghan, and Sydney Pollack in his final screen appearance prior to his death less than a month after the film's release. In its opening weekend the film grossed $15.5 million in 2,729 theatres in the United States and Canada and ranked at number 2 at the box office, only kept off the top spot by the heavily advertised *Iron Man*. Internationally it grossed $60 million which gave great exposure for *It Is Time for a Love Revolution*. The soundtrack also featured James Morrison, Noel Gallagher, Kanye West and Frankie Goes to Hollywood amongst others.

'Bring It On' was played on the ninth episode of the fifth season of the drama series *One Tree Hill* and 'I'll Be Waiting' was featured throughout on the 2008 Brazilian soap opera *Beleza Pura*.

To kick off the album Lenny performed 'Bring It On' on *The Letterman Show* in February as he made plans for his tour. He also released the second single from the album, 'Love, Love, Love', in February, and the video for the track premiered on MTV's TRL later in the summer on June 3rd. The video itself shows just Lenny and various blended images of him crossing over through psychedelic swirls and special effects, with dances also interspersed through the imagery; it's a simple video but it's effective and suits the track. The tour listing Lenny chose brought together all his past fan favourites as he blended in his new material, with most opening shows now kicking off with 'Bring It On'. The tour also had a promotional kick attributed to it which started things off during a nine-date club mini tour.

The 'Get on the Bus Tour' had winning tickets through the platform Myspace, and winners were treated to the 'Get on the Bus with the Love Revolution' club tour by travelling on the Kravitz-designed custom tour bus and becoming part of the artist's tour family on the road. They also received full backstage access to the live concert event. The winners started on the tour in Santa Monica, then California, before ending in New York City on February 1st. The promotion was running so that at each stop on the tour they would pick up one contest winner and their guest and they rode on the Love Revolution bus until the end of the tour. Another treat for the fans on the promotion was Steven Tyler of Aerosmith also joining the bus after he guested at The Orpheum Theatre in Boston. The winners were featured in the YRB February Edition alongside Lenny in a magazine pull-out. The photo shoot itself took place on the stage of the Electric Factory in Philadelphia.

With the promotional side of things well underway and the tour itself ready to go, Lenny was given a setback. He had been suffering from a series of infections since mid-January and the illness had now developed into severe bronchitis. On February 11th 2008 Lenny was admitted to hospital in Miami. The illness forced the planned tour to be disrupted and Lenny had to postpone the Canadian dates and also his trip to Europe. He also was forced to cancel a planned tour of South America which affected dates in Colombia, Mexico, Brazil and Argentina.

Lenny resumed in May when he played the Rock in Rio festival. It was the third edition of the Rock in Rio event and took place in Lisbon Portugal on May 30th and 31st and June 1, 5th and 6th. Lenny played his set on May 30th; he played alongside Amy Winehouse, Ivete Sangalo and Paulo Gonzo. The concert followed on from the Rock in Rio festival after the huge success of Rock in Rio 3 in Brazil; Roberta Medina decided to organise a festival of the same stature in Lisbon but the decision to maintain the same name was controversial with many in Brazil calling for it to be renamed to Rock in Rio Tejo after the Tagus river which runs through the Portuguese capital. Lenny arrived in Germany in June now fully recovered and back to his live best. He played at Olympia Halle in Munich followed by Palladium in Cologne before heading to Sweden and then Finland where he played in Helsinki at the Hartwall Arena. He played one date in Estonia before he again travelled to Russia, where he played in Saint Petersburg and Moscow at Maxidrom, the annual international musical festival organised by Radio Maximum station. Lenny headlined on June 14th alongside Bi-2, Brainstorm, Dolphin, Boombox and Noize MC.

The tour continued gaining fantastic reviews throughout June. Lenny and the band rocked Ukraine, Lithuania and Latvia before playing at the 02 Arena in Prague. He next played Switzerland, where he performed at Open Air St. Gallen, the annual music festival which is held near the city of St. Gallen and has been going since 1977. It is one of Switzerland's biggest and longest-running open air festivals and is attended by more than 110,000 people each year. A few days later Lenny played Rockin Park festival 2008 again in Holland. Joining Lenny this year were Anouk, Counting Crows and Starsailer. With the festival circuit in full swing Lenny played Rock Werchter at Festival Park in Belgium on July 3rd before BBK Live in Bilbao. The spinoff Rock in Rio events continued when Lenny rocked the event in Madrid on July 6th. Lenny played in the beautiful town of Pistoia Italy at Pistoia Blues Festival on July 13th, the event this year featuring Jethro Tull, Commander Cody, The Last Standing, Nine Below Zero, Tommy Emmanuel, Andy Timmons, Deep Purple, Watermelon Slim, Hot Tuna, Johnny Winter, Dickey Betts & Great

Southern and John Lee Hooker Jr. with Lenny headlining. The town of Pistoia is rich in history and heritage and the annual event is showcased in stunning surroundings in the historic town; the region is fantastic for tourists within easy reach of Florence, Pisa and those interested in the arts and the renaissance.

While in Italy, a day after Pistoia, Lenny was honoured in Milan. He was awarded the prestigious key to the city in a special toast ceremony for his work with the United Nations Millennium Campaign to end world poverty. The campaign was set up in October 2002 and aimed to increase support to achieve the Millennium Development Goals and seek a coalition of partners for action. The Millennium Campaign targets intergovernmental, government, civil society organisations and media at both global and regional levels. The campaign involved many aspects over the years through social media in music and stand up. Lenny's work was recognised at the event in Milan.

Next Lenny continued through Europe playing The Montreux Jazz festival and then the Moon and Stars event on July 17th. He next played The Nuke Festival where he closed the event on July 19th. Starting in 1999 in Austria The Nuke Festival was held until 2009 by the concert agencies Musicnet and Nova music, Nova Rock Frequency and since 2015 by the Arcardia Music Agency. The name came about as the very first concert was held in front of 3,000 visitors on the grounds of the Zwentendorf nuclear power plant. Since 2015 the location changed around before settling in Graz. Now annually over 35,000 people attend the event. The festival prides itself on having a wide range of musical diversity and no one genre is prevalent.

A day later Lenny continued rocking the festival circuit: he appeared at Festplatz in Germany before the tour continued to Hungary. The set list was now settled within the tour and he usually played the following: 'Bring It On', 'Always on the Run', 'Dig In', 'Fields of Joy', 'It Ain't Over 'Till It's Over', 'Dancin' Til Dawn', 'Another Brick in the Wall Part 2', 'Billie Jean', 'Be', 'Stillness of Heart', 'I'll Be Waiting', 'Where Are We Runnin?', 'American Woman', 'Fly Away' and 'Are You Gonna Go My Way'. Moving through August Lenny and the band played in Greece, Macedonia and Croatia before again appearing at Smukfest Skanderborg

Festival in Denmark. The event was attended this year by over 40,000 spectators.

Returning to the UK Lenny performed at The Carling Academy in London before hitting the UK festival circuit. He played two nights at V festival on August 16th and 17th 2008, the first at Western Park in Stafford and the following date at Hylands Park in Chelmsford Essex. Alongside Lenny at this year's event were The Verve, Kings of Leon, Amy Winehouse, The Feeling, Girls Aloud, Squeeze and The Stranglers. The 'V' represented the Virgin Group, with the event being sponsored by Virgin Media. The festival was originally televised by Channel 4 from 1997 to 2013, predominantly on their sister station Channel 4 Music. MTV later televised it from 2014 to 2015, and in 2016 it was then televised by Channel 5 in the UK. It was later announced by Richard Branson in October 2017 that V Festival would be discontinued and a new festival would replace it. From 2018 a new festival called Rize was held on the same weekend as the V Festival but only at the Hylands Park venue in Chelmsford Essex. Tickets went on general sale on 7 March for V and by 10am they had completely sold out; in fact they sold out in 90 minutes with extra tickets being made available on 26 June. Lenny performed in front of over 100,000 people. Lenny next played at Marlay Park in Dublin which was later home of the Longitude festival, which started in 2013. The tour resumed in Canada in October.

Lenny released his third single from *It Is Time for a Love Revolution* in November, 'Dancin Til Dawn'. The video for the song was released around the end of October 2008. It shows Lenny performing the song in a bar and features him walking on a street. The bar is actually the GoldBar, a favourite lounge hang-out of his in New York. Later a new video was created and released and is a lot more explicit: it shows a woman grinding on a bed before Lenny joins in while holding a camera and photographing. It appears pretty pointless apart from being blatantly explicit. The reissued video was directed by Jean-Baptiste Mondino who also had a hand in the Madonna video 'Justify My Love' and this is in familiar territory. The song itself has a pounding beat with swirling electric guitars in the background. The main focus on the track is Lenny's vocals, which are pushed to the foreground; this makes it a stand-out track and gives it a superb quality feel. The tour continued through Canada in October 2008 with concerts in Toronto, Halifax, Montreal, Regina and Calgary.

Next Lenny planned another tour. It was what he loved to do and *Love Revolution* was still performing well in all his strong territories. The run however suffered another postponement as Lenny again suffered bronchitis, and under the strict instructions of his doctor he was told to rest before hitting the tour circuit again. His newly planned Let Love Rule Tour, or LLR 2009, was rescheduled into 2009 as plans were made. At the start of that year, before the rescheduled tour dates were announced, Lenny followed in the footsteps of his mother as he made his acting debut to critical acclaim in January 2009, no doubt a debut she would have been proud of, *Looking Back on Love*...

Photo © Romain Paquini

Photo © Laurent Valay

Gregory Town

In January 2009 Lenny made his feature film acting debut in the movie *Precious*. The movie premiere was shown at the Sundance Film Festival. Sundance usually takes place annually in Utah and has around 40,000 attendees, which makes it the largest independent film festival in the United States. It's held in Park City, Salt Lake City Utah, as well as at the Sundance Resort itself, and the festival is a showcase for new work in film from American and international independent filmmakers. The festival comprises competitive sections for American and international dramatic and documentary films, which consist of feature films, short films and a group of out-of-competition sections which include NEXT, New Frontier, Spotlight, Midnight, Premieres, and Documentary Premieres. The film *Precious* made its debut here in 2009 and featured Lenny in the movie as he played Nurse John McFadden. It was Lenny's first film he had starred in that wasn't a standard cameo appearance. He had appeared in *Zoolander*, *Rebelde* and *The Diving Bell and the Butterfly* previously but all as cameo appearances and not acting roles as such.

    Precious was directed and co-produced by Lee Daniels while the script was written by Geoffrey S. Fletcher. The movie was adapted from a novel in 1996 called *Push* by Sapphire. The film stars Gabourey Sidibe, Mo'Nique, Paula Patton, and Mariah Carey. The film marked the acting debut of Gabourey Sidibe who portrays a young woman struggling against poverty and abuse. She went on to star in future films such as *Tower Heist* in 2011, *White Bird in a Blizzard* in 2014 and *Grimsby* in 2016; also from 2010 to 2013 she was a main cast member of the Showtime series *The Big C*. The film actually premiered without a distributor, but became acclaimed at both the 2009 Sundance Film Festival and the 2009

Cannes Film Festival. At Sundance it won the Audience Award and the Grand Jury Prize for best drama, as well as a Special Jury Prize for supporting actress Mo'Nique. After the screening in January 2009 Tyler Perry announced that he and Oprah Winfrey would be providing promotional assistance to the film and it was then released through Lionsgate Entertainment. *Precious* won the People's Choice Award at the Toronto International Film Festival in September and the film's title was changed from *Push* to *Precious* which was to avoid confusion with a 2009 action film which had just been released, also called *Push*. *Precious* was also an official selection at the 62nd Cannes Film Festival. Lionsgate later gave the film a limited release in North America in November and it received largely positive reviews from critics with the performances of Sidibe and Mo'Nique, the story, and its message being generally praised. In the film's opening weekend in limited release it grossed $1.8 million which put it in 12th place at the box office. A year later the film had grossed over $47 million domestically, ranking no. 65 for 2009, recouping its $10 million budget, and making it a classified box office success. Later in the year Lenny appeared on *The Ellen Degeneres Show* and talked about the movie prior to its official release. He spoke openly about how pleased he was with it and talked about his daughter Zoe, who was now 21. He also spoke about being single and joked that it was practically impossible for him to meet anyone, as Zoe screens the girls he meets. Ellen also showed a tweet of Lenny in the shower that he had recently posted on Twitter.

Lenny returned next to the funk album he had been playing around with for many years. He spent his time between studios working through songs; in fact many of the songs date back to 1997. While taking a break from constant recording in New York Lenny recorded some tracks at the studio of Allen Toussaint in New Orleans.

Allen Toussaint was one of the most influential figures in New Orleans and remained so for many years. As an American musician, songwriter, arranger and record producer he recorded and worked from the 1950s through to his death in 2015. He was often described as 'one of popular music's great backroom figures' and had a string of hits and recordings to his name which many musicians recorded; these included 'Java', 'Mother-in-Law', 'I Like It Like That', 'Fortune Teller', 'Ride Your Pony', 'Get Out of My Life Woman', 'Working in the Coal Mine', 'Everything I Do Gonna Be Funky', 'Here Come the Girls', 'Yes We Can Can', 'Play Something Sweet', and 'Southern Nights'. He was also a producer for hundreds of recordings, among the best known of which were 'Right Place, Wrong Time', by his long-time friend Dr. John (Mac Rebennack), and 'Lady Marmalade', by Labelle. The studio itself, named after Allen, Sea-Saint Studios, was a music recording facility located at 3809 Clematis Street in New Orleans, and it was owned by Allen Toussaint alongside A&R man and publishing agent Marshall Sehorn. The studio was in operation for thirty years from 1973-2005. Tragically it was destroyed during Hurricane Katrina which was another reason why Lenny would have participated in the fundraising events. Many musicians recorded at the studios including Paul McCartney, Paul Simon, Patti LaBelle, Joe Cocker and Elvis Costello as well as Lenny.

Lenny spent a lot of time during this period in the Bahamas. He released a video on his Twitter page that showed him working on one of the songs for the new planned album, the track 'Super Love'. The song was being worked through at GTS studios in the Bahamas, or Gregory Town Studios. There was another video released that shows him working on another track titled 'Life Ain't Never Been Better Than It Is Now', again at GTS. As he worked through with various songs and ideas the original album title was changed again from *Funk* to *Negrophilia* but Lenny still wasn't completely happy with the title and said at the time that it felt like something else, something different, so the name was again shelved for the time being.

Lenny's life during this period was one of reflection and taking up as much of the Caribbean lifestyle as he could. He resided in an Airstream trailer on a beach in the Bahamian isle of Eleuthera. He confessed his life was so simple that he had just a few shirts and a couple of pairs of jeans and simply hosed them down, hung them and rotated them. The area was always attractive to Lenny in and around Gregory Town; his mother grew up nearby so it had the family connection. He enjoyed the simple lifestyle, no keys, no shoes and no money, although the latter wasn't far away if he of course needed it. It was also a good time for Lenny to reflect. *Greatest Hits* managed to win him his fourth consecutive Grammy Award and *It Is Time for a Love Revolution* had some of Lenny's best debut positions and opening sales weeks worldwide in years, sitting alongside his best critical reviews since *Lenny*. Sales numbers at this time were also impressive: albums *Let Love Rule*, *Mama Said*, *5* and *Greatest Hits* had been confirmed to have achieved a sales status high enough to be certified at the next level within the sales threshold, if that mattered to Lenny, and of course as he continued to create more music and more albums these sales would increase. In addition to writing and producing all of his own work Lenny had also the albums he produced for other artists, with some of these also reaching great success and continuing to do so. To this point he had scored three top 10 albums in the US, while having reached number one in both the UK and Australia; he had achieved hits in virtually every continent: North America, US and Canada, Central America, Europe, United Kingdom, France, Germany, Spain, Scandinavia, South America, Brazil, Argentina and Colombia, Asia, Japan, Oceania, Australia and New Zealand, and Africa Republic of South Africa. He was now considered one of the most successful and best-selling rock artists of his time with sales of over 40 million albums alone worldwide, and not including singles and video releases. He also had the accolade of his numerous charity albums and collaborations with artists of a wide range of genres. He had participated in numerous soundtracks such as *Reality Bites* in 1994, *Austin Powers: The Spy Who Shagged Me* in1999, and *Bad Boys II* in 2003. He contributed tracks to *Power of Soul: A Tribute to Jimi Hendrix* and *Goin' Home: A Tribute to Fats Domino*. The 2004 album *The Unplugged Collection, Volume One* featured a live version of 'Are You Gonna Go My Way' from Lenny's critically acclaimed *Unplugged* session, as well as countless other career highlights through touring and brilliant performances he had achieved to this point. If Lenny was now taking time to reflect in the serenity of the Bahamas then it was completely understandable, though of course the peace and change of surroundings just filtered through to songs and recording - for Lenny the music wouldn't stop.

The making of his album, eventually titled *Black and White America,* was filmed, and used in various videos. It was later released as a documentary titled *Looking Back On Love*, which was directed by Grammy Award winning filmmaker and photographer Mathieu Bitton.

After hearing various reports of people reacting to President Obama Lenny had thought of the new title for his album; he had been listening to racist views that disturbed him and thought of the title *Black and White America,* and that stuck: it would become the name of his new album. Lenny's studio which he had built, Gregory Town Studios or GTS, was about 500 sandy yards from his trailer and this gave him real freedom; he was in nature and feeling no pressure to record to any sort of deadline. It was almost like he was accepting that the less you have, the happier you are, and this mindset suited Lenny during this time. The studio on the Eleuthera Island in the Bahamas sits on a 110-mile-long sliver of land 50 miles east of Nassau and working here Lenny had a sense of being back to his roots. His grandfather, who he was very close to, was born on an island called Ingua which is the most southern Bahamian island and closest to Cuba. Lenny would spend summers and Christmas and holidays down there and now he was living the simple life, but with the added bonus of having his recently refurbished state of the art studio a stone's throw away.

Lenny refitted the studio with equipment he had collected throughout his career. Lenny's love for and pursuit of the sounds he wanted had made this collection a worthy one, which started when he was initially recording at Henry Hirsch's waterfront studio in 1985. His love of analogue had started all those years ago from a need to escape from the processed sounds of the late 80s. The big gated drums and everything sounding unnatural never worked for Lenny, and he stayed true to his sound. Over the years with his close association to Henry Hirsch he would be introduced to certain gear, whether vintage or otherwise, and if it worked well and he liked the sound Lenny would purchase it. All these various pieces of gear were now fully installed in one place, giving Lenny his own personalised play area for his own musical perfection.

The studio Gregory Town Sound, or GTS, started initially as just a simple garage which Lenny had built to protect some of

126

his belongings during the hurricane season. The studio has a ranch style design and concrete over the top to create a type of cantilevered roof. Lenny absolutely loved the studio and along with all his gear he had been collecting over the years it allowed him to be creative in an environment he loved. Lenny worked his interior design skills when developing the studio and brought in a Miami-based acoustician and designer, Ross Alexander. Ross Alexander had been working on studio set ups since 1981 so was able to work out what Lenny could and couldn't do with his initial ideas. Lenny would then react and change his ideas to suit the planning. It was a balance between Lenny's design and not interrupting any sound quality that he needed.

The building itself is 1,800 square feet and has a 400-square-foot control room with a 600-square-foot studio. There is also a bathroom, lobby, machine room and an air-conditioning closet. The planning for Gregory Town Sound was done on a computer program. Lenny's recording style was also factored in to the design of GTS; he had two drum kits installed so he could record uninterrupted and switch back and forth. The studio has a large window facing the water and houses a baby grand piano, a number of guitar amps and many other instruments which Lenny would utilise depending on the track or the mood. One thing that was an issue was that of power; as this was the Bahamas the standard power needed to run a state-of-the-art studio was well below par, and they had to install an extensive power system because the Bahamas' electric is not terribly reliable. Henry Hirsch had a wraparound Helios console that was once owned by Abbey Road studios and actually used in Studio 1, and Lenny had this installed; it's this that gave Lenny the Stones and Zeppelin sound, which started around the time of the *Circus* album. Some of the gear that Lenny finally installed he had purchased nearly 20 years prior; he had bought various pieces of equipment and stored them, even though at the time he wasn't financially secure, and this equipment was now refitted.

It also allowed Lenny to indulge himself in his own sound. For years, and even on the demos tapes he presented to record companies all those years ago, he was described as a mix of styles, too much of a mix, too black, too white, a bit Hendrix, a bit

Lennon, a bit Zeppelin, a bit Gaye, a bit Mayfield, a bit Wonder, a bit Prince. All these individuals however had their own sound which was unique to them. But Lenny's sound was a mix of all of these great artists, it was what he was, his influences had penetrated him and this is what came out of him, it was almost like he wasn't in control, the songs flowed that way. Here, when you reflect back on his past albums and his past work, it was this that actually was the Lenny Kravitz sound. Prince had the Minneapolis Sound, and maybe Lenny's unique blend of all the past greats highlighted above was always 'The Gregory Sound'.

Lenny was delighted with the work that he did with Ross Alexander. Gregory Town Sound allowed him to get the exact sound he was looking for and it enabled Lenny to have a balance. He now had his studio on the beach with his trailer that allowed him to create and record in freedom. Being in the middle of nowhere living a simple life is conducive to writing, but he also had a big house in Paris which allowed his more extravagant side to be fulfilled: here he had ballet, opera, museums, great food and fashion.

With the album name decided, *Black and White America* was scheduled for release on August 22nd 2011 in Europe and August 30th 2011 in the US. Significantly it was Lenny's first release outside of Virgin records. Virgin Records was sold by Richard Branson to Thorn EMI for a reported US$1 billion, around £560 million. The sales had a special non-competition clause that would prevent Richard Branson from setting up another recording company for five years, giving the new merger time to settle without any direct competition. It was reported that Richard Branson sold Virgin Records to fund Virgin Atlantic Airways, which at that time was coming under intense anti-competitive pressure from British Airways. After being acquired by Thorn EMI, Virgin launched several subsidiaries like Realworld Records, Innocent Records, blues speciality label Point Blank Records, and Hut Records, and continued signing new and established artists like Korn, Tina Turner, Depeche Mode, The Rolling Stones, The Spice Girls, The Smashing Pumpkins, We Are Scientists, The Kooks, Meat Loaf, Placebo, Janet Jackson, Daft Punk, Massive Attack, The Chemical Brothers, Gorillaz, Paula Abdul, Mariah

Carey, and N.E.R.D. Lenny signed with Roadrunner records for the album, via Load and Proud. Roadrunner concentrates primarily on heavy metal and hard rock bands. It was initially founded in the Netherlands and imported US heavy rock bands; when Lenny signed to them it was a division of Warner Music Group and based in New York City.

This was a significant step for Lenny Kravitz. Other major artists had over the years broken out and were showing that you could take control of your own albums without having to sign long recording contracts as were common in the past. The industry was changing and changing fast. The standard chart was broken, shattered, fragmented into break off charts within genres, and it made a number one record a thing of the past. Media was changing and platforms were popping up all over the place: YouTube, Spotify, iTunes, Apple Music, Tidal and countless others were offering music 'direct' to the listener. If you were already established, with a huge army of fans around the world, your options were huge. George Michael had battled against his long-term deal, and ultimately lost in court, and Prince had just a few years earlier been involved in a very public battle with Warners, which he ultimately won; Prince set a precedent for future artists like Lenny who had the ability musically and logistically with their own teams and studios to run things more themselves, independently. The preferred choice was shorter deals, maybe even one album and then move around, ultimately setting up your own label and doing it internally. The days of a record company rejecting an album because they didn't feel it was commercial enough were coming to an end, especially for established true musicians like Lenny Kravitz. This intervention and record company and management control over what was released would be left for the X-Factor/Whatever Country's Got Talent generation. This music and the people involved would continue to dominate the charts with the same tired manufactured processed songs; talent shows spitting out year on year forgettable singers and acts that frankly are a world away from the talents of Lenny and others mentioned who were breaking away.

Aside from the manufactured drivel mentioned above the music industry for serious artists and musicians like Lenny was in need of deep change, and as an offering had to evolve to stay relevant. It had always consisted in a basic form of companies and individuals that earned money by creating new songs, setting up live concerts and making audio and video recordings, the compositions and sheet music. Within this you had music publishers, music producers, recording studios, engineers, record labels, retail and online music stores and various performance rights organisations. There were also those that organised and presented live music performances, the sound engineers, the booking agents, the promoters and the music venues themselves, including road crew. The list goes on: there were also a range of professionals who assisted singers and musicians with their music careers, particularly newly signed artists who had signed long term deals that were common back in the day, when the industry was more about just airplay and sales of a raw product i.e. vinyl, cassette or CD. These consisted of talent managers, artists and repertoire managers, business managers and entertainment lawyers. It worked its way into satellite, Internet radio stations, broadcast radio and TV stations. Then of course a record company would have so called 'pluggers' to gain radio airplay and work with radio stations around the world to try and get their artists played at peak times, to gain the songs exposure - it was a huge growing list of management that was expensive to organise and each part of the music industry had to fit in place to create hit records and lucrative tours; but things were changing, and key artists were no longer satisfied in giving away huge percentages to accommodate the above, especially when you could go direct to the people that mattered.

All of the above came at a cost and was one of the reasons a major record company looked at 'long term deals' with major artists so they could develop them in line with all these factors. This also meant lower percentages for the artist, a key point, and one that the record companies justified - from their perspective these deals allowed them to fund the expensive search and development of future talent. In short, the established acts were funding the search for new talent.

So why would someone in the position of Lenny Kravitz be tempted or interested in a long-term contract, one that could dictate an album and what went on it; who had the right to tell Lenny Kravitz what could, and should, go on one of his albums? He had his own team in place for making the records, his established engineers, his trusted band that he had had from the start. And also, the industry was changing in terms of sales: year on year the digital side of sales were getting stronger - in 2014 digital sales were 71% of all music sales in the USA, direct music to the consumer.

Lenny also now had his own studios, GTS, and they were perfectly set up and designed to his taste, designed by him and engineered to create the sound he wanted, his signature sound. It's no surprise at all that he would go for short deals and ultimately set things up to take complete control of all aspects of his work, and future recordings. For Lenny the future wasn't just clear; it was *Black and White*.

Photo © Chrystelle Roujean

Photo © Laurent Valay

Black and White

The first single from *Black and White America* was released on February 20th 2011, 'Come On Get It'. The video is shot in New York and shows the band being set up to perform behind a chain link fence as passers-by gather and wait as things get set up. The crowd are mainly young, college aged, and Lenny is seen walking to the stage, plugging his guitar into the amp and kicking off the show as the crowd go crazy. He is seen with a much shorter cropped haircut. The video is clearly appealing to the younger crowds, who maybe are in need of some rock & roll as opposed to the chart dominating misogynistic hip-hop which flooded the mainstream. Lenny was clearly happy with the track as it became the opening song on his next tour; it fits well into the list of openers that Lenny has had in the past and is a great track to kick off his concerts, full of the energy and bite that Lenny has always been renowned for, especially live.

This was a busy period for Lenny. Not only was he preparing to launch his tour in support of *Black and White America* but he was also cast in the forthcoming movie *The Hunger Games*, which was to be filmed between May and September 2011. The movie was directed by Gary Ross, who called Lenny for the role of Cinna. Cinna is the fashion stylist assigned to Katniss Everdeen, played by Jennifer Lawrence, as she prepares to take part in the Hunger Games. His unique designs play an integral role in her performance in the Games. The casting however caused some surprise, especially for those who were familiar with the book the film is based on, being an adaptation of Suzanne Collins' best-selling trilogy. Lenny was an established hard rock and roller but was cast in the role of the sensitive, sympathetic stylist Cinna, not the first choice in the heads of those who may have been familiar with the book. Lenny explained that he didn't go after the role but instead it was offered to him: he was working on *Black and White America* when he received a call from Gary Ross who asked Lenny if he would like to do the movie. Gary had seen Lenny in *Precious* and thought he could bring a sensitive side to the character in mind. Lenny admitted at the time he had no idea what *The Hunger Games* was so downloaded the book that night and read through it. He rang Gary Ross the next day and agreed to do it. They agreed that Lenny's character would be toned down from the original book, to make him more subdued in keeping with fashion icons. Filming started and the movie was released later, in March 2012.

Lenny's tour in support of his new album, the Black and White America Tour, kicked off with a mini supporting role similar to that he did with Aerosmith. Arguably one of the biggest touring bands in the world were kicking off their next world tour, entitled The 360° Tour. U2's 360° Tour was the band's next venture staged in support of their 2009 album *No Line on the Horizon*. The tour was scheduled to play stadiums from 2009 through to 2011, the main feature of the tour being the unique stage as the band played on a circular stage similar to Prince in 1988 during his Lovesexy Tour. It allowed the audience to completely surround the band on all sides. To allow the stage set up to be configured a huge structure was installed, 'The Claw'; this was a four-legged structure built above the stage which allowed the sound system and a cylindrical expanding video screen to sit on top of it.

At 164 feet (50 m) tall, it was the largest stage ever constructed for a touring band. The tour was a major source of income for the band, as their music sales had been in decline, and every date was completely sold out within minutes of going on sale. Also because of the unique structure the venues the band played at could increase on the standard capacity, which allowed records to be broken in over 60 venues as capacity could increase by 25% in some cases. As expected with such a huge tour and all the promotional elements that went with it the first shows, which featured Lenny, were widely anticipated and a great platform to launch Lenny's own tour. The tour was also in connection to the 20th anniversary of the band's release of *Achtung Baby* and so

135

heavily promoted around this; it was a kind of nostalgic event highlighting the longevity of the band. The tour as expected hit records and became reported at the time to be the highest-grossing concert tour ever. It allegedly achieved $736 million in ticket sales. It was also reported that they had the highest-attended tour, with over 7.2 million tickets sold.

The day before Lenny played his first concert on his five date U2 tour he released his second single from *Black and White America*. Again produced, written, arranged, composed and performed by Lenny, 'Stand' was released as a single and an iTunes download on June 3rd 2011. The song was written about a close friend of Lenny's who had an accident and was left paralysed from the waist down, who later recovered. 'Stand' was covered by the cast of the television series *Glee* during the third season of the show. Again, reviews of the track were favourable and many felt it was the best new release of the summer, a perfect pop tune that was instantly planted in your head after one listen. The music video for 'Stand' was directed by Paul Hunter and premiered on VH1 on July 14th. It's a bizarre video to say the least, especially if you are not familiar with what the video is supposed to be in connection to, and it's widely similar to Outkast and 'Hey Ya' in its feel. Lenny plays the part of three separate characters, but he primarily plays the part of a presenter called Bart Billingsworth who was a host of a crooked game show called *Run For Your Money* from the USA, a typical game show type of programme; Lenny also plays the game show house band drummer named Bubba Washington and the lead singer who was Desmond Richie, probably instantly obvious if you are familiar with the gameshow but completely lost on those not so familiar. Lenny still clearly had the acting bug and was willing, or complicit, to play parts within the video as opposed to his normal role playing music or scene setting, which was what his videos were like on the whole. The voiceovers are clear throughout the video as well and interrupt the song as it's played, as they talk over the track. The main theme of the video is that the host and his female assistants are switching the prizes behind a curtain after the audience member has chosen a number, so that the audience only win low value prizes, and as the game goes on the drummer sees the scam and pushes a button to open the curtains, and all is revealed. The hosts then make a run for it with the prizes as the audience mobs the stage. It's a video attempting to be humorous and going for good fun and comedy but doesn't in any way have anything to do with the song itself, which is a great catchy pop song in relation to fighting against the demons inside you and standing strong and positive when you feel the world is against you.

The first concert for Lenny in support of U2 started at Qwest Field in Seattle on June 4th 2011. Lenny's setlist was around 50 minutes and started with his new single 'Come On Get It', followed by 'Mamma Said', 'It Ain't Over 'Till It's Over', 'Let Love Rule', 'American Woman', 'Fly Away' and ending with 'Are You Gonna Go My Way'. It was essentially a greatest hits set with his new song as the opener. He played on June 7th at 0.co Coliseum at Oakland, 14th June at Del Mar Racetrack in California and the final two concerts both at the Angel Stadium in Anaheim on the 17th and 18th June.

Lenny released 'Rock Star City Life' on July 7th as the third single from the album but he chose to perform 'Stand' on *The Late Show with David Letterman* on August 30th before he commenced the Black and White America Tour, this time as himself and not attributed to anyone else.

'Rock Star City Life' was another step for Lenny reaching out in other directions; he was feeling generous and with a surge of 'Giveaway Generosity' he offered the single as a free download, for 48 hours. The single was also the last song he wrote in the recording sessions for the album so it was a good promotion just before the release of the album a month away, in August. Lenny during interviews prior to the release said that the process of making *Black and White America* was longer than previous albums he had done; he admitted prolonging it and constantly going back and reshaping it. He also said that because of this he was 100% happy with the finished product. Once he had completed 'Rock Star City Life' he said he knew the album was done, it was time for it to be released.

On August 29th Lenny finally released *Black and White America*, his ninth official studio album. The album as previously stated was widely reported to be his long-awaited funk studio album which was originally intended for release before *Baptism*, but Lenny decided on the last-minute songwriting sessions and changes. Unusually the album would have many singles connected to it, highlighting that Lenny was searching for a hit single from it to gain exposure: he produced six singles in total and had them released through 2011 and into 2012. This made sense from a commercial perspective as many of Lenny's past hits had been picked up through TV, film or other media which instantly made them successful, along with the attributed album; even third singles became successful through this and the album instantly benefitted from the exposure. By rolling out many singles he cast the net widely in the hope that something would get picked up through other media.

The album was released through Roadrunner Records/Atlantic Records under joint label Loud & Proud. Lenny talked a lot about the writing of the album. He had previously explained the name change, in connection to hateful things he had heard and read in connection to President Obama, but he also said that one particular song, 'Push', was actually from a dream that he had; he openly said that many of his songs come to him in dreams that way and 'Push' came to him while he was waiting to perform a scene in the movie *Precious*. Lenny recalled that on the night of Barack Obama's first election win he was in a freezing city in Canada and he responded to the news by hitting some R&B and political minded tracks. 'Push' has a Beatles type feel; it's a horns-driven number about positivity in spite of hardship and was inspired by his family's early struggles for acceptance. Lenny claimed he was in total shock at the news of Obama, that he had lived to see an African American president, it was amazing to him. He said of the album title track that he wished for things on the Internet, the negativity that was out there in connection to the new president, the stuff he was reading, to simply go away.

The cover features Lenny as a young boy, and is a nod to him being the child of an interracial couple who got together during the civil rights movement; the cover therefore is a personal one and also fits the themes within the album connected to society, unity, love and peace. Lenny even has a peace sign on his face. The actual picture was taken by Lenny's dad when he was in second grade.

It's within the schoolyard of P.S. 6 on 82nd Street and Madison Avenue. There was a sort of school bazaar going on and his mum had a little booth where she was painting kids' faces. Lenny found the photo about six months before the album was finished and it reaffirmed the album itself to him so he decided to use it. Lenny stated the kid in the picture was how he was and not contrived in any way - lots of ruffled sleeves, necklaces, bracelets and peace signs. That was who he was and it fitted the album perfectly.

Lenny again stated on the making of the album in interviews how the peaceful location of Eleuthera had helped him, and how it let him focus purely on his art and nothing else, the simplicity of the location. He also spoke of how each of his albums has its own identity, and that they are individual pieces that can't be compared as such; the only difference in Lenny's mind to his albums are that they are new.

Lenny was now embracing different media. As well as having a new label he released the second single 'Stand' on Facebook, and the video was released on iTunes, YouTube and Vevo on June 6th. Again, as before, the critical reception for *Black and White America* was positive and many wrote that it was Lenny's best record in years, completely enjoyable and full of instantly catchy tunes. It's an album that is Lenny again making a cohesive musical statement and once more showcases to the masses what an illustrious musician Lenny Kravitz is in welding together the fusion of rock and funk. It's another coming together of the two themes, a melting pot of funk, soul, rock and other born-in-the-USA genres. The themes take on biracial qualities, with civil rights and the equality movement, and a hope for change in society in general. Lenny again has strength when he is most personal and all of the 16 songs on the album have their own fortitude within Lenny's wide repertoire of musicianship. He was also reflective and autobiographical within the album; he mentions in 1963 his white father marrying a black woman and when they walked down the street they were in danger; it's heartfelt and deeply personal with the overall message that harmony is needed beyond the divisions of black and white.

Of course, as with every Lenny Kravitz release, the similarities with past work from other established greats were thrown into the writing mix, and some even described it as playing Lenny Kravitz Bingo where you listen and try and guess the style and artist that Lenny was trying to replicate; the majority however were in favour, and agreed that *Black and White America* was his most experimental album for many years. It's an album that has strength, depth and is completely uplifting in its message, blending the social, spiritual and sensual. It's also a blacker album than Lenny had written for a long time; he has funk well and truly tightened within many tracks with the embellishments of horn and slap bass; the synth is also buzzing through with interjections of strings. He also cameos two of rap's biggest names on the album: Drake and Jay-Z, showing an ability to reach out and cross that divide that many artists in Lenny's position simply wouldn't. Lenny here is embracing the threat and entwining it to make it his own; what better way to showcase his own talents as a true multi-instrumental musician than to bring in two rap artists, therefore blurring the lines between genres, something Lenny Kravitz completely excelled at, the ability to embrace everything musically and blend it in, to make his own.

Black and White America is an album that could have been easily released during the mid-1970s alongside Stevie Wonder's *Songs in The Key of Life;* the feel of the album and the vintage blend Lenny uses would have made it sit well amongst the funk rock albums of this period coupled with the interracial social and political messages for change. Most songs on the album are also quite short so nothing is over exposed and works well through to the next; each track is around 3.5 minutes and as always with Lenny Kravitz the hooks and chorus have an instantly recognisable feel to them. As has happened many times before the album was initially more commercially successful on the European market than in the US. It charted in the top ten in various countries, including in Germany where it went straight in at number 1. In the US it debuted initially at 17 but as Lenny toured the album would clearly pick up more ground as he again hit the road in support of the album. He also played some mainstream shows as the year came to a close in preparation for the tour itself.

Lenny appeared on mainstream TV again on *Late Night with Jimmy Fallon* in New York on September 1st, where he played 'Rock Star City Life' on the show. He next flew to London and played BBC Radio 2's Hyde Park concert on September 11th. The show was featured live on Radio 2 and broadcast in the UK and all over the world. The next night, still in London, he played at The Box in Soho before leaving and preparing for a much larger venue altogether.

He released his next single, 'Black and White America', on the 19th, a day before he played the Rock in Rio festival on September 20th 2011. This time Lenny had the performance recorded, and it was released on DVD later in 2012 with the same name as the lead single for his new album. The 'Come On Get It' DVD had the following live track listing from Rock in Rio: 'Come On Get It', 'It Ain't Over 'Till It's Over', 'Mr. Cab Driver', 'Black and White America', 'Fields of Joy', 'American Woman', 'Always on the Run', 'Believe', 'Stand', 'Where Are We Runnin?' 'Fly Away' and 'Are You Gonna Go My Way', and the encore, 'Let Love Rule'. While still in South America Lenny next performed at Personal Fest in Buenos Aeries Argentina. The Personal Fest is held annually in Buenos Aires and has been going since 2004. It was named after its main sponsor, Personal. It was originally held in the neighbourhood of Puerto Madero, and since 2006 has been held at Club Ciudad de Buenos Aires. More than 55,000 people attend the festival each year. Also playing the same night as Lenny was Chilean singer Beto Cuevas.

Lenny travelled to Europe next to continue his tour where his popularity was always huge. He started in France in October before one show back in England on October 27th at HMV Apollo Theatre in Hammersmith, before returning to mainland Europe. He played for four nights in Germany but was forced to return later in the year to meet demand. He played Poland, Lithuania, the Czech Republic, Croatia, Austria, and three shows in Italy all completely sold out before returning again to Germany at the end of November where he played again at Olympiahalle in Munich.

Continuing on with the tour Lenny played three shows in Switzerland at the end of November; he played on the 24th in Geneva and the 25th and 26th in Zurich. The concert on the 25th was at the Energy Star Night concert which was formerly the Energy Stars for Free event held annually in Zurich. It has been organised since 2003 by Energy Zurich and since 2010 together with Energy Bern and since 2012 with Energy Basel. The event was broadcast live by ProSieben Switzerland. The name 'free' is connected with the concert tickets themselves which are not actually on sale, but are raffled or given away by various lotteries. Energy Stars for Free was first launched in 2003, and the event had around 1500 spectators. The second edition in 2004 grew to around 4500 visitors in the Maag EventHall. Since 2005 the concert series takes place in the Zurich Hallenstadion and each year has over 13,000 spectators. In contrast to the Energy Fashion Night, the Energy Stars for Free takes place in autumn/winter. In October 2016, the organisers announced that the event will be renamed Energy Star Night. Also performing at this year's event was Ed Sheeran amongst others.

On December 1st 2011 while on mid tour Lenny was honoured with one of the highest cultural awards in France. He was made an Officer of the Ordre des Arts et des Lettres by French cultural minister Frederic Mitterrand in Paris. Translated as 'Order of Arts and Letters' the award is an order of France which was originally established in 1957 by the Minister of Culture. Its supplementary status to the Ordre national du Mérite was confirmed by President Charles de Gaulle in 1963 with its purpose being in recognition of significant contributions to the arts, literature, or the expansion and growth within these fields. The French government guidelines stipulate that citizens of France must be at least thirty years old, that they must respect French civil law, and must have significantly contributed to the enrichment of the French cultural inheritance to be considered. Membership is not however just limited to French nationals, and recipients include numerous foreign luminaries which this year included Lenny Kravitz, whose record sales and indeed popularity in France was huge. The Order has three grades: Commandeur (Commander) which has a medallion worn on the necklet; this has up to twenty recipients a year; Officier (Officer) which has a medallion on the ribbon with a rosette on the left breast; this has up to sixty recipients a year; and Chevalier (Knight) which has a medallion worn on the ribbon on the left breast; this has up to 200 recipients a year. Lenny was awarded the Officier award. Lenny said at the time he was 'particularly touched' to receive the award in France as his success in the country pre-dated his success in the United States, and he still enjoys great record sales in the country today. Other American recipients of the award include Martin Scorsese, George Clooney, and Bob Dylan.

Lenny returned to the US in December to kick the off the *Black and White America* tour with a performance on the *X Factor* on December 8th. He performed 'Push', 'Rock Star City Life' and 'Are You Gonna Go My Way' on the show, and he got a thumbs up from Simon Cowell after the performance, which is clearly important.

The documentary that was recorded during the making of *Black and White America* was now released, on December 12th 2011.The title of the documentary was *Looking Back on Love*, and it was directed by the critically acclaimed photographer and filmmaker Mathieu Bitton. Born in Paris, Mathieu Bitton has an enviable body of work connected to some of the most prestigious talents in music and film; he has designed posters and album art for Prince, Jack White, Sting, Miles Davis for the *Bitches' Brew* 40th Anniversary Edition box set, Marvin Gaye, Jane's Addiction, Bob Marley, Quincy Jones, James Brown, George Clinton, Earth, Wind & Fire, Iggy Pop, Lou Reed, Dolly Parton and of course Lenny, amongst many more.

Interested in music and the visual arts from an early age, Mathieu's first musical idol was the French singer and musician Serge Gainsbourg, who is arguably one of the most influential French pop stars of all time. He was instantly interested in the art of music and the impression it created, anything shocking and controversial that blended the picture both aurally and visually. Paris also held a wealth of inspiration for him, being surrounded by architecture, culture and the arts. At a young age Mathieu started collecting albums and film posters, building a huge collection of inspirational material that influenced him to follow a path into photography and film. He became a huge Prince fan and in particular described the album *1999* as life changing. Prince for Mathieu encompassed everything he was looking for both musically and visually. He eventually got to see Prince in 1986 and described it as a complete one-man visual spectacle of all the past greats he loved but had never seen, that of Marvin Gaye, James Brown, Jimi Hendrix, Sly Stone and even Mozart all rolled into one.

Following the path in search of a break into the music and film industry Mathieu made his way to LA to pitch his talents. He met and worked with Quentin Tarantino on several designs and posters for his company and his reputation soon grew as a major talent within film; it wasn't long before Mathieu Bitton became one of the most sought-after directors, photographers and designers in the industry. Over the years that followed he has amassed as art director and designer over 850 albums, books and posters, creating and designing countless corporate, band and event logos. He worked as a soundtrack designer on many films including Martin Scorsese's *The Departed*, Michael Bay's *Transformers* franchise, Kevin McDonald's Bob Marley documentary and the Aretha Franklin documentary *Amazing Grace*, as well as countless other pieces of quality work within film, design and photography.

Mathieu had known Lenny since childhood and the pair had always stayed in touch; however, they became professionally reacquainted before the making of *Black and White America*. The film was discussed and three months were set aside for the documentary showing the making of the album at Gregory Sound. It's a superb piece of quality work and follows the journey of the making of the album brilliantly; it's in depth and looks at the sessions as they happen, capturing Lenny perfectly and sympathetically as he creates the album. It's a full rock production which includes interviews and discussions about Lenny's creative process, showing the actual recordings of the songs themselves. It also shows Lenny's long-time collaborator Craig Ross, as well as Zoe Kravitz and New Orleans trombone legend 'Trombone Shorty'. It's a sublime insight not just on Lenny's work but also Lenny himself, the man. It demonstrates Lenny's full dedication to his craft, and more importantly captures it without feeling intrusive; it follows the evolution of the album through to completion and along the way we hear Lenny reflect on his love of life as well as great humour. Mathieu captures it skilfully and his back-seat approach to the film reveals the journey almost as a video diary; it's guided gently and expertly. Visually it is stunning and all of Mathieu's past wealth of knowledge for photography and film are shown here; it's perfectly lit and captures light and angles in a brilliant and flawless way, and of course the setting and backdrop of Gregory Sound is stunning. The result is a first-class documentary that opens the door to fans and music lovers on an artistic process normally hidden from view. Mathieu Bitton captures a simple thing within the film, that of the creation of music, making it a great visual experience. He makes Lenny shine, capturing his talent and creativity, and he becomes both fascinating and intriguing throughout the documentary. It's a must have for fans.

Continuing on with high profile TV shows Lenny played on *The Tonight Show with Jay Leno* on December 13th and two days later on *Jimmy Kimmel Live* where he played 'Come On Get It' and 'Always on the Run'. These were three high profile shows to get things kicked off.

After the Christmas break Lenny started his tour of the USA at Wang Theatre in Boston. The standard set list was 'Come On Get It', 'Always on the Run', 'American Woman', 'It Ain't Over 'Till It's Over', 'Mr Cab Driver', 'Black and White America', 'Fields Of Joy', 'Stand By My Woman', 'Believe', 'Stand', 'Rock and Roll is Dead', 'Rock Star City Life', 'Are You Gonna Go My Way', and 'Let Love Rule'. Of course, things changed as the tour progressed but this was the main backbone of the setlist. He next played Music City Hall in New York before moving on to Detroit and Chicago. The tour continued in February to fantastic reviews in Minneapolis, Denver, Phoenix, Oakland and LA where Lenny played at The Nokia Theatre on February 16th 2012. On February 26th Lenny performed at the Daytona International Speedway and several of the performed songs were carried live on Fox for the Daytona 500, which is the opening race of the 2012 NASCAR Sprint Cup season. The final concert on this leg of the tour was at Fillmore Centre at Miami Beach Florida. Lenny and the band then travelled to Australia to continue through March and rock down under.

The Australia leg kicked off in Melbourne at Myer Music Bowl on March 17th and 18th, and Lenny then moved on to

Wollongong, Sydney and Brisbane. The final concert on this leg of the tour was held in Hobart on March 28th before the tour then moved on to Japan beginning in April.

Shortly before the last date of the Australian leg of the tour *The Hunger Games* was released on March 23rd 2012 featuring Lenny playing the role of Cinna in the movie. The movie earned a reported $408 million in the US & Canada, and $286.4 million in other countries, making a for an impressive worldwide total of $694.4 million. It achieved the largest worldwide opening weekend for a film not released during the summer or the holiday period, earning $211.8 million, beating that of *Alice in Wonderland* which held the previous record of $210.1 million.

No doubt after heading to the cinema to watch *The Hunger Games* Lenny played at the 55,000 capacity Tokyo Dome on three nights, March 4th, 6th and 7th, to over 165,000 fans; he then played at the Giebun Arena in Nagoya on April 9th and at Grand Cube in Osaka on April 10th making Australia and Japan hugely successful for him.

In May 2012 Virgin records released a special 20th anniversary edition of *Mama Said*. In addition to the original songs the double-disc reissue features six non-LP B-sides and 15 unreleased tracks, which include rough demos and unreleased remixes. It also featured several previously unreleased tracks and serves as a fantastic representation of Lenny's talent and his recording process. The new listing was as follows - Disc 1: 'Fields of Joy', 'Always on the Run', 'Stand By My Woman', 'It Ain't Over 'Till It's Over', 'More Than Anything in This World', 'What Goes Around Comes Around', 'The Difference is Why', 'Stop Draggin' Around', 'Flowers for Zoe', 'Fields of Joy (Reprise)', 'All I Ever Wanted', 'When the Morning Turns to Night', 'What the Fuck Are We Saying?', 'Butterfly', 'Light Skin Girl from London', 'I'll Be Around',' Always on the Run (Instrumental'), 'It Ain't Over 'Till It's Over (12" Remix Instrumental)', 'It Ain't Over 'Till It's Over (12" Extended/Dub version)'; Disc 2 contained more bonus material: 'Riding on the Wings of My Lord (Rough Demo)', 'It Ain't Over 'Till It's Over (Home Demo)', 'What the Fuck Are We Saying? (Home Demo)', 'The Difference is Why (Home Demo)', 'Riding on the Wings of My Lord (Funky

Vocal)', 'Riding on the Wings of My Lord (Instrumental)', 'Framed', 'Lying', 'Crying (Instrumental)', 'Stand by My Woman (Instrumental)'. The second disc also contained live tracks, these including 'Stop Draggin' Around (Live in Rotterdam)', 'Always on the Run (Live in Rotterdam)', 'Fields of Joy (Live in Rotterdam)', 'Stand By My Woman (Live in Rotterdam)', 'More Than Anything in This World (Live in Rotterdam)', 'Always on the Run (Live in Kawasaki, Japan, July 1991)', 'Stop Draggin' Around (Live in Kawasaki, Japan, July 1991)', 'What the Fuck Are We Saying? (Live in Kawasaki, Japan, July 1991)'.

The set was a must for fans and the release got it right; this was an anniversary set that wasn't just simply remastered and then reintroduced to the market - for true fans that didn't work, it wasn't going to be attractive. This was a set of pure quality and one that gives new and bonus material with superb quality live tracks; it was worth the addition to any sets a collector of Lenny Kravitz would want. It also set a perfect representation to his talents by showcasing the raw and uncooked tracks that give a glimpse into his recording process and the development of songs and writing in the studio.

Lenny played the Mawazine festival in Morocco on May 25th as part of his tour. The festival is held annually in Rabat, Morocco and features many international and local music artists. The festival is presided over by Mounir Majidi, the personal secretary of the Moroccan King Mohammed VI and founder and president of Maroc Culture which is the cultural foundation that organises Mawazine and other events. The festival is huge and regularly attracts around 2.5 million people, making Mawazine the largest festival in the world after Donauinselfest in Vienna. It has around 90 acts on 7 stages and it has the highest ratio of attendees per stage in the world. Mawazine is also important for Morocco itself: it is is one of several events which are intended to promote an image of Morocco as a tolerant nation, and a post on the event's website declares that the goal of the festival is to promote Rabat as a city open to the world. It has nonetheless sparked controversy and many in the country are against it, especially those who are traditional in their beliefs; some Moroccan politicians have criticised the event for its openness and for in their view 'encouraging immoral behaviour'. It has also been criticised for allegedly having financing by Moroccan state-owned companies or private companies whose only client is the actual Moroccan state. That aside a huge number of key acts have performed at the festival including Whitney Houston, Mariah Carey, Rod Stewart, Stevie Wonder, Alicia Keys, Shakira, Justin Timberlake, Jennifer Lopez, Enrique Iglesias, Christina Aguilera, Rihanna, Ricky Martin, Pharrell Williams, Placebo, Maroon 5, The Jacksons, Sugababes, Chic, Bruno Mars, Kylie Minogue, Ellie Goulding, Sting, Julio Iglesias, Robert Plant, Cat Stevens, B.B. King, Carlos Santana, Elton John and Deep Purple. Lenny played his tour setlist at the event finishing his set with a full-on audience participation to 'Let Love Rule' in fitting with the venue and perhaps some of the controversy surrounding it.

Lenny released 'Superlove' from the album on May 29th 2012. The track was remixed by Tim Bergling aka Avicii, the Swedish musician, DJ, remixer, and record producer. The track was released as a digital download in the United Kingdom and charted in the UK, Belgium, Hungary and the Netherlands. Lenny later released a music video for the song to YouTube in August. The video shows a jogger arriving home dressed in 80s type running gear, shorts and top, and finding a Sony Walkman cassette player on the path outside his house; the tape has 'Superlove' written on it and the man takes it indoors. He then puts it on and the remix track starts; he then goes through a 1980s type dance in his lounge before being transported forward in his head, in a dreamlike sequence, to clubs and a hedonistic world before popping out of his dream at the end to find a man standing in front of him just when he was about to kiss a girl. Lenny does not appear anywhere in the video.

Spain was next for the *Black and White America* tour, where Lenny rocked through on May 27th, 29th and 31st performing at The Coliseum at Corunna. Before the final Spanish concert in Barcelona Lenny took a short flight to Portugal to play Rock in Rio Lisboa 2012, the breakaway concert connected to the main Rock in Rio festival. Lenny headlined the event on 1st June; other headline acts for this year's event were Metallica, Linkin Park, Stevie Wonder and Bruce Springsteen, who closed the 2012 event on the 3rd. Lenny again played the festival circuit while on his own tour and hit dates through June in Europe. He played Norwegian Wood on June 15th, the Oslo festival named after the Beatles track and formed in 1992; Lenny played alongside Brian Ferry, Tom Petty, Sting and James Morrison at this year's event. The next day, still in Norway, Lenny played The Bergen Calling Festival in Bergen. The location is a spectacular one for this festival, located at the medieval Bergenhus Fortress & Castle in Norway. Lenny played another two dates on his own terms before playing again at TW Classic Festival in Belgium; he played Rock in Rio in Madrid and again at North Sea Jazz in Rotterdam.

In July Lenny brought the *Black and White America* tour to a conclusion. Staying in the Netherlands Lenny played Bospop Festival, The Moon and Stars festival and The Gurtenfestival in Switzerland. He rocked Musilac in France, Rock in Roma in Rome, Paleo Festival back in Switzerland and finally in Germany, where he played at Stimmen Festival in Lorrach in front of around 30,000 fans, the festival being held in the main square of the city.

The album and tour had been very successful for Lenny; the period he took to reflect on his life and his forward outlook had worked well. On the album he again had established himself as a hugely talented songwriter with an ability to blend all his inspirations and great American genres together into one Lenny Kravitz melting pot. His new recording studio had allowed him to record the album unhindered and without pressure: he was able to take his time, to listen to it back and to reflect on it. He added more things to it until he was completely satisfied with it, and only then was it released. It also had a personal theme to it and this played to Lenny's songwriting strengths. The tour that followed also was hugely successful with Lenny playing sold out dates throughout the USA, Europe, Australia and Japan and as before he included the festival circuit, gaining more followers to his ever-increasing army of fans. He also now had a major feature film successfully playing around the world which he had co-starred in, and another *Hunger Games* movie was being talked about. Lenny Kravitz had every reason to *Strut*.

Photo © Laurent Valay

One in the Chamber

Lenny spent the first half of 2013 carrying on with his acting career. He was on the set of the second *Hunger Games* movie, soon to be released, and he also filmed and appeared in *The Butler*, an American historical drama film that was directed and produced by Lee Daniels. The film is inspired by Wil Haygood's *Washington Post* article titled 'A Butler Well Served by This Election' and is loosely based on the real life of Eugene Allen, who worked in the White House for decades. The main actor in the movie is Forrest Whitaker, who plays Cecil Gaines, an African-American who is a witness to several key political and social events in the 20th century, during his 34-year tenure serving as a White House butler. The film also stars Oprah Winfrey, John Cusack, Jane Fonda, Alex Pettyfer, Cuba Gooding Jr., Terrence Howard, James Marsden, David Oyelowo, Vanessa Redgrave, Alan Rickman, Liev Schreiber, Robin Williams, Minka Kelly, Mariah Carey and Clarence Williams III as well as Lenny. It was the last film produced by Laura Ziskin, who died in 2011. Lenny played the role of James Holloway, a co-worker of Cecil's at the White House. The movie was scheduled to finish in August 2012 but was delayed due to Hurricane Isaac. On its first weekend of release the film debuted at number 1 on the box office and grossed $24.6 million, and it topped the box office in North America for three consecutive weeks. It eventually made a combined total of $167.7 million, from a budget of $30 million.

On June 8th 2013 Lenny took a break from filming and appeared at CMA Festival in Nashville, or Country Music Association, where he played a relatively short set of greatest hits: 'Fly Away', 'Always on the Run', 'American Woman', 'Are You Gonna Go My Way' and 'Let Love Rule'. The CMA began in 1972 as Fan Fair; the event is huge and draws over 400 artists and celebrities who hold autograph sessions and perform in one of the many concerts offered throughout the festival. The event now stretches to four days and has an estimated attendance to have exceeded 250,000 people at various ticketed events and in the free areas. It attracts visitors from over 40 different nations, and all 50 states in the US. Lenny then continued with filming for the next film in the *Hunger Games* series. It was announced that Gary Ross, who directed the first film and cast Lenny, would not be returning for the second film, the reason given being due to the tight schedule. Several names were quickly drafted in to replace Gary Ross including Bennett Miller, Joe Cornish, Francis Lawrence and Juan Antonio Bayona. In April it was announced that Francis Lawrence would be offered the director position for the film, and a couple of days later it was reported that Michael Arndt, who had previously worked on *Toy Story 3* and *Little Miss Sunshine*, was in talks to completely re-write the script for the new movie. On May 24, 2012, the film was officially renamed *The Hunger Games: Catching Fire* and Michael Arndt was confirmed as the new writer of the script. It was reported at the time that Michael Arndt was paid an alleged $400,000 a week for re-writing the script. Filming commenced well and with the new script complete, Lenny completed his second film of the year.

The Hunger Games: Catching Fire was released on November 15th 2013 in Brazil. Shortly after on November 20th it was released in Finland, Sweden and Norway. It was released in the UK on November 21st and a day later on November 22nd in the US. Again Lenny played Cinna in the movie. The film once more was hugely successful and benefitted from a large advertising campaign prior to release. The film set records for the biggest November opening weekend and biggest three and five-day box-office totals, surpassing the first film's box office totals. It ranks as the 14th-highest-grossing film at the domestic box office and the highest-grossing film at the domestic box office of 2013. It also became the first 2D film since *The Dark Knight* in 2008 to top the yearly box office. The numbers, as with the first film, are huge; it grossed over $865 million worldwide which made it the fifth-highest-grossing film of 2013.

Lenny retreated to Gregory Town Sound, as he had done for *Black and White America*, to record his next album over the months through 2014. He took a short break to perform at AT&T park, or Oracle Park, the home of the San Francisco Giants, the city's Major League Baseball franchise, but other than that he bedded down in the Caribbean to concentrate on his next album, which he scheduled for release in September, to be titled *Strut*. Again, Lenny employed his usual team to assist him in creating his new album, but as ever Lenny is foremost on the record and commands the sound on nearly all the tracks. Lenny was listed as playing lead and background vocals, electric and acoustic guitars, Mellotron, bass, drums, chimes, hand claps, ARP string ensemble, mini-moog and even wine glasses. Craig Ross played acoustic and electric guitars and handclaps while James 'D. Train' Williams provided background vocals alongside Cindy Mizelle and Tawatha Agee. Dave Baron was listed as synthesiser programming with Harold Todd on saxophone, Ludovic Louis on trumpet, Darret Adkins on cello, David Bowlin on violin and Kenji Bunch on viola. Tom Edwards was the recording engineer. The rest of the listing for the album is for people who provided handclaps.

Lenny released the first single from *Strut* on June 24th 2014, 'The Chamber'. 'The Chamber' is pure glitter-ball rock & roll and is a great illustration of Lenny's studio ability and songwriting craft to create a catchy tune that sounds like it's been around for years. The music video for the song was shot in Lenny's apartment in Paris. It was directed by Anthony Mandler who as a music video director has mostly worked with Rihanna. Together they have to date worked on sixteen music videos throughout her career, beginning with 'Unfaithful' in 2006 and most recently 'Diamonds' in 2012. The video also features Dutch model Rianne ten Haken. It's a superb video and acts out the song perfectly. Lenny is obviously happy with his newly sculpted torso as this is in abundance throughout.

Before the release of the album Lenny released his next single, 'Sex', on August 6th. The guitar riff on the song is pure dirty glam rock and fits perfectly with the title. The video shows Lenny on stage performing the song flanked by two dancers; they are constantly interrupted however by those filming the performance and directing it, a priest and a series of nuns, who stop proceedings to give costume changes and direction. A blonde woman enters as the video goes on brandishing a whip and a goat also makes an appearance; the video ends with a nun replacing one of the dancing girls and the priest removing his collar - it's a bizarre piece of theatre but works well with the song.

Released on September 23rd 2014 *Strut* is Lenny's tenth studio album. Following on from the label release of *Black and White America* Lenny moved further forward with more control and ownership as he released the album on his own newly set up Roxie Records, the label's name obviously in tribute to Lenny's mother. The distribution of *Strut* was through Kobalt Label Services. The Kobalt Music Group is an independent rights management and publishing company that was founded back in 2000 by CEO Willard Ahdritz. It acts primarily as an administrative publishing company and importantly does not own any of the artists' copyrights, which makes it very attractive for artists like Lenny Kravitz. It also offers label services. The company had also developed an online portal to provide royalty income and activity to artists, allowing them to manage their rights and royalties directly. In December 2011 Kobalt bought Artists Without a Label, or AWAL, which is a digital distribution and label services company, and as a result Kobalt immediately gained access to AWAL's network of digital retail partners, these including amongst others iTunes, Amazon, Spotify, eMusic, Rhapsody, 7Digital, Beatport, Deezer and Nokia. This gave Kobalt permission to supply advanced data analytics to clients. In basic terms the business model that Kobalt had gave much larger percentages to the artist than a standard recording contract of the past.

Strut produced five singles which were released both in 2014 and into 2015. It had excellent reviews with many linking *Strut* to a golden period in Lenny's studio craft, an artist in control and at his peak. It's an album of supreme studio technical ability and full of swagger, and it's another demonstration of Lenny's replica sound of funk and dirty soul. The very title gives the listener an early nod as to what's ahead on the album and his intentions are clear: he wants to swagger, he wants us all to move and groove with him and immediately we are in and involved as the opening track kicks into action. 'Sex' moves us straight into dirty, groovy territory - it's immediately obvious that we are not moving through social and political territory as we did on *Black and White America*. This is an album that stays clear of all of this and sticks to a clear principle, that of pure indulgence in the grooves. It's longer than average as well, sitting at 12 songs reaching 53 minutes, but the grooves are so infectious this is not an overplay, more a happy record flowing with rhythm.

It has its sultry tender moments on 'The Pleasure and the Pain' and 'Never Want to Let You Down' and also a cover of Smokey Robinson's 'Ooo Baby Baby'. The cover was a song written by Smokey Robinson alongside fellow Miracle member Pete Moore and was first released in 1965, when it became a hit for The Miracles for the Tamla Motown label and achieved a number 4 placing on the Billboard R&B singles chart, and reached number 16 on the Billboard Hot 100. It was covered by Linda Rondstadt in 1978 and was hugely successful, reaching number 7 on the Billboard Hot 100. It's a track that many had covered over the years including Ella Fitzgerald and Todd Rundgren. Many wrote that the track 'Frankenstein' was a track influenced by Bill Withers, but again aside from the search for what Lenny is allegedly trying to replicate it's an album dedicated to glam and disco, with each song having an individual style and unique twist within this area. Again, production is a key strength for this album with Lenny demonstrating his skill in getting the sound he wants in line with each track, but not so much to act as a diversion in the consistency of the album. He brings in big beats, dirty sex and weighted hooks and all sonically trashy where needed, and this works and makes it sound fun - it makes it a real pleasure to listen to. Again, the Lenny Kravitz funk, rock and soul pick and mix are blended to music hedonism; it's full of variety and gives a perfect balance between something that is brand new and yet sounds vintage and warm, like a reminder of a good memory from the past, when songs and albums were crafted and designed to be studied and enjoyed from start to finish, a musical journey as such. Lenny was one of the key artists that still believed in this, and as an individual was one of the best at it.

At this point Lenny had been around as a recording artist for over 25 years; he had produced album after album and with *Strut* he gave another first-class account of the ability he first showed all those years before. His vocals are as strong as ever on the entire record, distinctive and strong, and they carry perfectly each song as Lenny's harmonies and powerful mellow lead drive the tunes. The album has, more than any other for a long time with Lenny Kravitz, a notion of pure attitude; it's evident especially in tracks such as 'Sex' and 'Dirty White Boots'. 'New York City' is a long song, sitting at over six minutes, but it's a classic. 'Frankenstein' has great soul within it, and there is also a slight country feel to some of the tracks especially in some of the acoustic guitar work Lenny lays down. The tracks on *Strut* stay both radio and also club friendly: they will make people want to move and want to dance and, on that basis, Lenny once again succeeded brilliantly with his unique blend and fusion of all the styles he has in his locker. There is enough guitar in the album to please rock fans and enough soul to enhance Lenny's vocal delivery.

Strut is a very solid album in the Lenny Kravitz discography; it's a pure pleasure, it's unapologetically fun and it gets better from multiple listens. The songs on the album come across as a glam mix of 80s outtakes and even have the vocal delivery in this vein. It has the ability to even sound like it was discovered in a studio somewhere from the period and re-recorded. Lyrically and in the content Lenny has much more sexuality and a dirtier feel than he had put on albums in the past; he had of course bits of sexuality but nothing as hardcore and blatant as on *Strut:* 'take your knickers down and give me that treasure' is not the type of line Lenny had delivered in the past. It was a new horny Lenny Kravitz and he was here to groove and party. The standard 12 songs on the album were the following: 'Sex', 'The Chamber', 'Dirty White Boots', 'New York City', 'The Pleasure and the Pain', 'Strut', 'Frankenstein', 'She's a Beast', 'I'm a Believer', 'Happy Birthday', 'I Never Want to Let You Down' and 'Ooo Baby Baby'. Target had a promotional album that contained two additional tracks, 'Lift Me Out of My Head' and 'It Won't Feel the Same', making it 14 songs. On iTunes there were two different additional tracks, 'Sweet Gitchey Rose' and 'Can't Stop Thinkin' 'bout You', showing that Lenny had plenty more songs to provide but for the main album kept the listing as he thought it should be without overbearing the structure of the initial album itself.

Lenny here was reinventing himself once more, evolving into a new direction; there were still heavy Led Zeppelin influences, but there are flashes of brilliance within *Strut* that are pure Lenny Kravitz with no exceptions. What's interesting is that artists like Lenny - and there aren't that many left - have the ability to raise their own bar, therefore often something released as brilliant as *Strut* is expected to be brilliant before you listen. Just looking at the cover and reading the song titles gives an early indication as to what's to come, but the surprise is in the new direction of grunge, disco glam and dirtiness that takes it forward from *Black and White America*.

A month after the release of the album Lenny released another single 'New York City' on October 21st 2014. The video for the song is no surprise; it's filmed as Lenny walks through New York and is done unannounced so that the general public are on the video with him; we see him getting recognised and kissed by girls on the street as he makes his way through. The video clearly fits perfectly with the song and maybe it was the only way to go, but ultimately it works perfectly.

Also in October Lenny kicked off his *Strut* tour starting at Olympic Park in Russia. The setlist for the tour as always changed as the tour progressed but the core songs were: 'Dirty White Boots', 'American Woman', 'It Ain't Over 'Till It's Over', 'Strut', 'Dancin' Til Dawn', 'Sister', 'Circus', 'New York City', 'Dig In', 'Always on the Run', 'Are You Gonna Go My Way', 'I Belong to You' and 'Let Love Rule'. He continued through Russia in October playing in Moscow and St Petersburg before the tour played in Finland, Belarus and Poland. Lenny at this stage in his career was a master of live performance, and the concerts were the perfect balance of rock showmanship and extravagant performance. The glam sound of *Strut* also brought a new dimension to the concerts and as always Lenny was able to intertwine the crowd pleasers within and around his new songs. Behind the band was a huge screen showing Lenny in black and white and various other shots as they blasted through the set. It was a show of pure energy and rock and roll; Lenny on this tour sounded better than ever and the band, the voice and showmanship of the performance were second to none. As the tour progressed more dates had to be added to meet demand.

In November the tour reached Germany where Lenny played two dates at the start of the month; he would return later as new dates were added. Also in November Lenny played in Italy, Austria, the Czech Republic and Switzerland before returning to Germany as the new dates sold out. Before November ended, he played concerts in the Netherlands, Belgium and France with all dates completely sold out to capacity. Lenny released 'Dirty White Boots' on November 11th from the album, the fourth single since release. A concert at Omnisports de Paris-Bercy in Paris on 23rd November was filmed and sections of this are on various streaming sites. Lenny played at additional five concerts in France, such was his popularity in the country, before he returned to England to play at Wembley Arena on December 6th. He played an additional two concerts in France before the end of December as demand was still in abundance for tickets.

Once the new year started Lenny launched his US leg of the *Strut* tour. He again played at AT&T in January before a short break when he started planning his next album, while still in mid tour. Lenny next played to arguably his biggest audience of his life, especially through TV, when he appeared at the Super Bowl halftime show on February 1st 2015.

The Super Bowl XLIX halftime show was performed at the University of Phoenix Stadium in Glendale Arizona as part of the Super Bowl XLIX final. It featured Katy Perry, Lenny Kravitz and Missy Elliott as well as other special guests. The halftime show was critically acclaimed, and the audience that watched the broadcast on NBC was estimated at 118.5 million viewers in the US and an additional 120.7 million worldwide, making it the largest ratings in the history of the Super Bowl, this number making it to date the most watched halftime performance of all time; in fact the halftime show was watched by more viewers than the game itself. It even won two Emmy Awards later on September 20.

Lenny returned in April at Sunfest 2015 in Palm Beach Florida. At this year's festival were Hozier, Eddie Money and Pixies as well as Lenny. Lenny had his trademark look well and truly down for his performances during this period: he wore his usual outfit, dressed head to toe in denim with his sporting aviator glasses. The sets around this time varied but for festivals Lenny showcased his extraordinary versatility and variety of styles. At first the band started as a standard four piece offering but as each new song came around Lenny would bring on another guest musician or two adding to the ensemble. He had a trio of female vocalists flanking him for 'Are You Gonna Go My Way' and they became dancers as well as backing vocalists for 'Stop Draggin Around'. The female element was enhanced even more when he performed 'American Woman', which looked like it could be the name of his band such was the female presence. Lenny was joined on bass by long-time accompanist Gail Ann Dorsey as well as returning drummer Cindy Blackman, now Cindy Blackman-Santana. The band also had a tight horn section consisting of trumpet and two saxophone players, which brought in lengthy jam workouts at the end of songs. 'Always on the Run' had this treatment as well as an electric piano solo from Craig Ross. Lenny mixed effortlessly the old with the new as well as showcasing an acoustic section, making things personal and at one with the crowd; the band and the performances for this tour were exceptional and Lenny had the whole concert timed to musical perfection.

On May 1st Lenny played at Beale Street Music Festival at Tom Lee Park in Memphis, a 30-acre sprawling park on the banks of the Mississippi river. Also performing at this year's event were Ed Sheeran, Paramore, Hozier, John Fogerty, Five Finger Death Punch, Wilco, Pixies, The Flaming Lips, Cage the Elephant, Ryan Adams, Band of Horses, St. Vincent, Slash, and Awolnation.

Lenny spoke during the tour in interviews and explained that once he finished a record he quickly moved on to the next; he told of a new album already advanced in the planning which would be released within the next year or so, and he said the material he had already written was very funky and raw, very psychedelic. He said how pleased he was with it, describing it as really, really good. He talked about making albums and about how he was still in love with album-making as an art form, especially his love for vinyl which is what he grew up listening to and became his love; it's what sowed the seeds for Lenny's initial retro sound and his love for analogue within his work. For Lenny this is why albums mattered: the journey you can take the listener on as you progress through. Here at 51 years old he felt in himself that he was a better performer now than he was in his early days of touring, and this was true and evident when watching his shows. His other interests were still also performing well, his Kravitz Design lines of fashions, interiors, and architecture were still keeping him occupied outside of music, and he launched a photography exhibition which was shown in Los Angeles, Paris and Germany - another exhibition even opened in Vietnam. Lenny's passion was always music but he loved to explore other art forms, including design, photography and film.

Shortly after Beale Street Lenny and the band played again at New Orleans Jazz and Heritage festival at The Fair Grounds Race Course. The festival attracts around 200,000 visitors, the peak of the festival numbers being achieved in 2001 when a staggering 650,000 people attended during Louis Armstrong's centennial celebration. Lenny played New York on May 5th and here he changed the opening song of the concert to 'Dirty White Boots'. He played a concert in LA before again returning to Europe, where demand again was huge. He landed in Germany for two additional concerts before he played at The Concert at Sea Festival in the Netherlands. The festival is held on the Brouwersdam, which is an area that forms a barrier across the former estuary known as the Brouwershavense Gat in the province of Zeeland. The festival was first initiated by a popular Dutch band named BLØF. The first festival held was in 2006 after a free pilot concert at that location had proved to be very successful in earlier in 2003. Initially the festival was just one day but from 2018 it became a two-day event attracting over 40,000 visitors each day.

Lenny again moved around the festival circuit while in Europe between his main shows. He played again at Rock Werchter in Belgium on June 27th; headlining as well as Lenny on the main stage at this year's festival were Hozier, Noel Gallagher and The Prodigy. The festival received the Arthur award for best

160

festival in the world at the International Live Music Conference and can host 88,000 guests daily, in fact around 67,500 combine all four days, which makes a total of around 149,500 visitors each year to the event. For the festivals Lenny played around 55 minutes to an hour with the following setlist: 'Dirty White Boots', 'American Woman', 'Mr. Cab Driver', 'It Ain't Over 'Till It's Over', 'Dancin' Til Dawn', 'Strut', 'Always on the Run', 'I Belong to You', 'Let Love Rule', 'Fly Away' and 'Are You Gonna Go My Way'. Heading back to France Lenny played in Paris at Festival Cognac Blues Passions and at the beautiful main square in Arras. Created in 2004 by France Leduc Productions the Main Square Festival rose to become one of the major music events of the country, attracting worldwide famous bands and stars alike. Lenny headlined the event on July 3rd, and also playing that evening were George Ezra, Hozier and The Script.

Still in France Lenny headlined the Beauregard Festival on July 5th. The annual music festival was first created in 2009 and was seen by 20,000 people; it takes place in beautiful surroundings at the Beauregard castle park in Hérouville-Saint-Clair in the Caen area. The Caen area itself only has one festival so it makes it very popular; it was renowned for being devoted initially to electronic music but that changed as its popularity grew. To make the event stand out and be popular the fictional character of John Beauregard was created and he is present on the posters of the eight editions that have taken place to this point; he is also used for all marketing purposes. The estate at the castle where the festival takes place is within 23 hectares of meadows and wooded areas located at the foot of a castle, and due to demand the site was enlarged from 2011.

Lenny's interest in interior design also expanded in this year. Kravitz Design Inc, which he founded in 2003, now expanded its portfolio and Lenny launched a range of furniture and lighting. This was a passion of Lenny's and was his main focus outside of music; it kept his creative energies going. The firm, still located in the Soho area of New York, followed the designs and ideas that Lenny had, reflecting his global lifestyle. He worked in collaboration with a Chicago based company named CB2, and the newly launched collection featured around twenty pieces of designed furniture which included lamps, wall decorations, rugs, pillows and furniture. Lenny said the inspiration for the collection came from the sleek glam of the 1970s New York club culture and the natural ease of the California music scene of the same period, the 1970s. The collection was inspired by his constant travels around the world and the company was growing steadily with launches of various designs that Lenny came up with. Kravitz Design itself had recently completed the interiors for the SLS Hotel South Beach in Miami. The new furniture collection went on sale in October but was made available to pre order earlier. Lenny said the collection was used to furnish his own homes in France, the Bahamas and Brazil.

Lenny continued on the summer festival circuit throughout July. He played Sporting Summer in Monte-Carlo, festival de Nimes, Festival les Deferlantes, The Montreux Jazz Festival and Moon and Stars in Switzerland, Festival Marés Vivas in Portugal, Palacio de Deportes de La Guía in Spain, Starlight Festival in Marbella and Hard Rock Rising at Barcelona before heading to Italy where he played two more festivals, Rock in Roma and Hydrogen anfiteatro camerini piazzola sul brenta. Lenny completed the successful European leg of the *Strut* tour with concerts in Sweden, Denmark and Poland before he returned to the USA in August to complete the tour. In Sweden Lenny had a wardrobe malfunction that hit the headlines: during his concert in Stockholm he squatted down mid song causing his leather pants to split, and as he wasn't wearing underwear he was quickly 'exposed' - which was caught on camera, and of course circulated.

The conclusion of the *Strut* tour came in September. Lenny played The Greek Theatre in Berkeley California, Allen Event Centre in Texas and Woodlands in Texas before the final concert held at Music Midtown in Atlanta. The tour as usual had been a great success and with *Strut* Lenny had reaffirmed his status as one of only a handful of worldwide stars that had an ability to produce quality albums almost entirely by themselves; his talent for creating engaging, exciting and original music with the sprinkle of past influences was still as ingenious as ever. Lenny was here moving into an iconic status, and his back catalogue of material and his constant sold out touring all over the planet confirmed this.

Despite his creative endeavours through his interior design company and his love for acting, Lenny's first passion was music and the creating of quality albums. He returned to the studio frequently during the *Strut* tour and had enough material to put together another album. Lenny returned to put finishing touches to it and to again plan a world tour. It was time once more to showcase his new material to his worldwide fan base, to rock the arenas to their foundations as only Lenny could, and to bring everyone together in his own mix of positivity. To *Raise Vibration*.

Photo © Chrystelle Roujean

163

Photo © Vanessa Favaretto

Back to the Wall

Two months after Lenny completed his *Strut* tour the music world was dealt a seismic shockwave. Prince, at just 57 years old, was found dead at his Paisley Park Studios on April 21st 2016. Lenny, as expected, was deeply upset by his friend's passing, as were millions of fans and the music world in general. Prince was rumoured before he died to be suffering from hip and joint pain, and he was on an intimate tour named the 'Piano and Microphone Tour' - as the name suggests this was just him and a piano performing around the world and alone. Many thought in hindsight that the tour enabled a more pain free performance, with it being just Prince at the piano, and so was easier for him. That said, the shows were brilliant and again showed how talented he was, to completely rewrite and perform his songs making them suitable for the piano. The concerts were praised consistently and gave a wonderful insight into him personally and within an intimate setting. Prince had scheduled two concerts in Atlanta on April 7th but the shows were cancelled with no reason at the time given. This was extremely rare, and fans and social media lit up with speculation; someone like Prince simply did not cancel shows, and when it was finally announced he had influenza this again raised a lot of questioning from fans around the world. This guy simply did not get ill; it was as if Prince in some respects didn't even age - his non-stop musical life was always moving, he didn't have children, hadn't been married for years, had a new backing band and had just released another brilliant album. He was now performing a world tour in a superb intimate setting and fans were reviewing it as the best Prince concert they had ever seen, so a sudden cancellation and then an announcement of influenza created worldwide speculation that something wasn't right. Lenny said at the time he was concerned, and he even speculated about knowing what his friend's real issue was - he said he knew what it was. The main thought at the time was that Prince was suffering from hip pain which was caused by years of performing; he was taking drugs to ease the pain but something somewhere had slipped through and he was now getting into trouble.

The shows were rescheduled for April 14th 2016, and he performed the two shows back to back. These sadly would be his last. After the shows he flew back on his private jet to Minneapolis; but during the flight Prince fell unconscious and unresponsive, and the flight was forced to make an emergency landing at Quad City International Airport in Moline Illinois. Receiving medical treatment at a local hospital, it was alleged that Prince was treated with a shot of Narcan and when conscious discharged himself to return home to Paisley Park. It was soon circulated and revealed that Narcan is an opioid antagonist used for the complete or partial reversal of opioid overdose. Although Prince made a couple of appearances in the week that followed there was still widespread concern, and on April 20th Prince's representatives called for help and contacted a California based specialist in addiction medicine and pain management, Mr Howard Kornfeld. Kornfield cleared his schedule and planned to meet Prince on April 22nd. In the meantime, he sent his son to Paisley Park who had flown in with buprenorphine that morning to devise a treatment plan for opioid addiction. On arrival at Paisley Park that morning Prince was discovered unconscious in an elevator. Emergency responders were called and arrived at Paisley Park, where they performed CPR, but a paramedic said he had been dead for about six hours and they were unable to revive him. They pronounced him dead at 10:07 am on April 21st 2016.

It was reported afterwards that there were no signs of suicide or foul play and a press release from the Midwest Medical Examiner's Office in Anoka County on June 2nd stated that Prince had died of an accidental overdose of fentanyl at the age of 57. It is not yet known whether Prince obtained the fentanyl by a prescription or through an illicit channel. It was quickly reported afterwards that Prince did not have a will and therefore his estate would be divided between his siblings; this to many was a complete shock - how could a musician who absolutely controlled every aspect of his musical life not have it taken care of after his death to his exact wishes? Prince controlled all his music, and he fought for that control; he fought to own it and it was inconceivable that he would not have provisions in place for it after his death. Lenny said of Prince that he was a beautiful person and a true friend. Of course their similar lifestyles of writing, recording and touring constantly took them around the world in different directions, but the pair when together were very similar, hugely gifted musicians able to produce music alone and unhindered.

Prince put simply was a true musical genius, a ground-breaking icon, one of the most influential musicians of all time and one of the most daring stage performers and prolific songwriters in history, and he was still creating ground-breaking albums and touring consistently right up to his sudden death. Lenny was devastated by his passing, and millions of fans and the music world mourned him deeply.

Lenny said of his next planned album that the whole thing was entirely conceived through his dreams: he would wake up with another song in his head while in the Bahamas and the song was born. As he continued to work on the album at his studios, Gregory Town Sound at Eleuthera, it was leaked that it was to be named *Raise Vibration*. It wasn't all dreams and music however: Lenny took some time off from the recording to take an acting part that he was offered when he appeared in season one of the American television musical drama *Star*. The series was created by Lee Daniels and Tom Donaghy for Fox and debuted in December 2016. The plot is focussed on three young singers who work their way through the music business leading to stardom. The series was set in Atlanta and contained original music and fantasy type sequences showing dreams of the future. The series co-starred Queen Latifah, Benjamin Bratt, Amiyah Scott and Quincy Brown. Lenny played the part of Roland Crane, who was a legendary rock star, and he features frequently throughout season one. Casting started around September 2015 with the pilot shot in December. It premiered a year later in December 2016, running through to March 2017 as season one, and it was viewed by around 6.71 million people.

167

Once the album was completed Lenny released the first two singles in quick succession, the first single, 'It's Enough!', being released on May 11th 2018. The video for the single was a powerful one and Lenny had it live-streamed over Facebook and YouTube. It highlights and brings together various pieces of news footage that cover every angle from protests on racism to same sex marriage. It was Lenny saying he had had enough of racism, enough of war and the destruction of the environment, and he was also calling out on the dishonesty of world leaders. It was a message of hope, of love outweighing power. Lenny released 'Low' as the second single shortly after, on May 25th, before setting off on tour. The video for 'Low' is superb and shows Lenny singing at the drums before being replaced by Cindy Blackman Santana towards the end. The video was directed by Jean-Baptiste Mondino and Lenny said that when Jean Baptiste heard the song he concentrated on the beat and built the concept for the video from there. The conclusion was a simple one, back to basics, black room, black drum set, black clothing; it's purely focusing on the groove and the space. It presents the song perfectly in its production and highlights the conversation taking place.

Prior to the release of *Raise Vibration* Lenny kicked off his tour in support of his new record in June 2018 starting in Germany, then moved on to the Czech Republic, Hungary, Slovakia and Poland. Again, the set list changed slightly as the tour progressed but in general in followed: 'We Can Get It All Together', 'Bring It On', 'American Woman', 'Low', 'It Ain't Over 'Till It's Over', 'Believe', 'I Belong to You', 'Where Are We Runnin?', 'Always on the Run', 'Tunnel Vision', 'The Chamber', 'Can't Get You Off My Mind', 'It's Enough' and 'Let Love Rule'. Through June Lenny played Austria, a return to Germany for two additional concerts, Belgium and Paris before he arrived back in England. Lenny played Manchester, Birmingham and Wembley where here he changed the set slightly and opened with 'Fly Away'. Visually the concerts were spectacular, with a raised section at the rear of the stage allowing for Lenny to stand and 'strut' along, while front left and right were former Bowie bass player Gail Ann Dorsey and of course Craig Ross.

168

From here Lenny opened the shows with 'Fly Away' as the crowds immediately became the backing choir; typically Lenny started raised at the back on the platform, a very similar visual set up to Prince on his Controversy Tour, but it worked perfectly as an opener. Lenny looked the complete star with his dark shades and leather jacket, as he stood raised and perfectly lit at the start the show, a rock god in front of his funky loyal disciples. His voice as always was superb and the sound carried perfectly to every section of the arenas Lenny played. During 'American Woman' a brass section was introduced, taking the sound in a different direction. Lenny here steered the song effortlessly into and through Bob Marley's 'Get Up Stand Up', bringing the band members on stage to seven plus Lenny himself. As expected, he introduced tracks from the forthcoming *Raise Vibration*, playing 'It's Enough' and the title track itself, intertwined with the usual classics which, as always with the way Lenny introduces the songs, sound fresh and current when live; a sign of a truly great song, and Lenny has them in abundance. One thing that Lenny Kravitz always enjoyed was basking in the adoration of his fans' love for him when performing live and, on this tour, he raised this even further: he soaked it up, posing for photos and even signing programmes that were handed up to him. Knickers were often thrown on stage, presumably by women but who knows? 'I Belong to You', 'Always on the Run', 'The Chamber' and 'Again' followed with first-class precision. In Manchester England Lenny even pulled a small child from the audience to join him on stage to another huge roar from the crowd; always an audience favourite for any artist. Lenny knows how to encore, and from the repeated chants of his name he returned to bask again in the glory leaving with 'Are You Gonna Go My Way'. The shows were full of energy and charisma and demonstrated once again what an incredible live performer Lenny Kravitz is, especially in concerts on his own terms surrounded by his own core fanbase, visually engaging everyone from the start with the usual incredible band that flanked him in all directions.

As Lenny continued the tour the reviews of Lenny's concerts were first class and with his ever-increasing back catalogue of quality live material the only real disappointment was what the fans didn't hear from their own personal favourites. The shows were timed to perfection and visually spectacular, showcasing all the musicians Lenny had around him, a stage full of talent and musical quality.

The band played Switzerland on June 27th before O son do Camino 2018 at Santiago de Compostela on June 30th. The summer was here and Lenny again would headline and appear at festivals throughout the world, now fully established as a bona fide headliner to any major musical gathering. Into July Lenny played Portugal and Spain where he played in Madrid and Barcelona before arriving in France, a country that has always had a love affair with Lenny since his debut. Lenny played five concerts and even returned for two additional ones later in July, such was demand. After the last concert in France on July 30th Lenny took a break through August with the much-anticipated album itself finally released on September 7th 2018.

Raise Vibration was an album Lenny was very pleased with, and he should be - it's one of his best and most consistent, and it stands proud as a musical statement to a musician at the peak of his powers. Lenny said the album felt good to make, it felt authentic to him and represented him at the time. In connection to the album Lenny signed a deal with BMG Rights Management for a new worldwide publishing deal to go with *Raise Vibration*. Previously BMG had acquired Kravitz's music publishing rights in 2013, as part of the deal with Virgin Music Publishing. Lenny played everything on the album with the exception of horns and the orchestra; Craig Ross engineered the record with Lenny as usual producing it.

Lenny really enjoyed the making of *Raise Vibration* and during the recording sessions felt completely immersed in it, especially as he was working on the music inspired through the dreams that he'd had. This was something Lenny wanted to pursue; he said he didn't have them every night but he had them a lot, and when he did, he would quickly record the basic concept, and then work on the song over the next few weeks until it was completed, just working it over time. He kept a tape player by his bed and when during the night inspiration took hold, he would record it and then go to the studio to continue the next day, or straightaway if it was something he didn't want to forget. Lenny acknowledged that these things are a gift and he felt it was his job to accurately represent what he was hearing.

Raise Vibration fell as Lenny's eleventh album and arrives at a time when he needs to prove nothing to no one; it's full of his musicianship and signature sound - funky bass and sensual vocal deliverance. There is an underlying message within the album as well: anthems to the political turmoil Lenny sees in the USA - 'Who Really Are the Monsters?' - and again he nods towards his former good friend in Minneapolis with a purple tinged electro-funk jam that has him chanting 'The war won't stop as long as we keep dropping bombs and start communicating' - even lyrically it's Prince, but Lenny isn't robbing any vaults: he has more than anyone earned the right to be here. The album naturally has its gentle side, as with all Lenny Kravitz albums; the gentle piano ballad 'Here to Love' is a yearning for harmony against segregation and seeing the light. His vocals here are superb and straight on point. On 'It's Enough' Lenny references the middle east in a Marvin Gaye type delivery, like 'What's Going On?', but again it's just a reference and the underlying groove is pure Lenny. The deeper meaning throughout the album that remains constant is that of questioning authority, and asking who is really in charge of the world today; the deep underlying message though is never delivered in a way that sacrifices any grooves or melodies. The messages are delivered simply and to the point but at no time does the brilliance of the harmonies, melodies and song writing suffer under the weight of any political references. Of course, as ever, many reviewers will pick up Lenny's usual influences and have written about them in the usual way; we also get a full-on sample as Michael Jackson adds in the background vocals to the track and single 'Low', but even this is nothing more to the ear than sounding like Lenny Kravitz and not some weak track that's added a sample to find a hook. Lenny uses it skilfully on the single and it's his sample from past work, work he was proud of as he and Michael spent time in the studio together. It's a dancefloor-ready track and perfect for remix that many have circulated in the usual way. In summary, *Raise Vibration* is one of the best albums Lenny has ever produced; it's packed full of surprises and it's immensely intelligent.

It's been three decades on from when Lenny released 'Let Love Rule' and again we see a wonderful display of talent, blending and fusing together rock, soul, funk, and psychedelia. As the record industry gets ever boxed in with unimaginative trash regurgitated out from the *X Factor* generation, Lenny again displays an ardent caveat for quality with rock, soul and funk. It could, if you're a music critic, be not white enough; it could be not black enough; and of course it could be an album that Lenny will get criticised for as sounding too much like his past influences, as he did on *Let Love Rule*. This though thirty plus years on would be ridiculous to write, but it continues to be the case. The album again is a statement that this sound is one thing and one thing only, it's a Gregory Town Sound, it's Lenny Kravitz. It's a message that is evident through his entire career; he effortlessly unites all the key parts and the key message remains the same as it did three decades ago - it's about love. He said that he was offering vibrations of peace, love and unity and this is evident the most in the tracks 'Raise Vibration' itself and 'Here to Love'. With 'Raise Vibration' Lenny demonstrates again a balance in lyrical messages and melody, a balance of love and peace, of unity and world harmony that perfectly blend within the funky cool. Lenny Kravitz knows how to create an album properly, the ebb and flow, the rise and fall involved in the journey to make it cohesive, and with 'Raise Vibration' he again raised the bar for himself and those around him. A confidence and professional assurance combined with his unique blend of funk rock enhanced with his earnest beliefs in making the world a better place; it's full of promise and musically reassuring.

A couple of days after the release of *Raise Vibration* Lenny appeared again at Hyde Park in London for the 2018 event. The tour then moved to the USA leg starting in Atlanta - and it's here that we catch up with Lenny Kravitz within the pages of this book. Although this book is coming to a conclusion one thing is for certain: Lenny Kravitz is not. He has proved to be a true artist in every sense of the word and shows no sign of stopping or slowing down, - and long may that continue.

This book is also a challenge to critics: its purpose is to highlight the achievements and the musical skill of Lenny Kravitz in a world where musical skill is considerably weak. Artists like Lenny Kravitz should be celebrated; longevity and consistency is key, and it's this that puts Lenny at the top of the tree when it comes to producing new music. It's easy to listen to a new Lenny Kravitz album and try and guess who each song sounds like but this still seems to be the favoured method in which music critics refer to his records. His reviews have been written this way time and time again over the years and it now feels tedious and frankly boring to read. Lenny from day one was never shy about his influences: he openly embraced them, and took them on, whipping them into a funky rock fusion within his own unique musical blender. The very fact that he is compared to and sometimes sounds like other artists is precisely the point; he sounds like so many, and so many of the greatest artists of all time, that it is this that makes him unique - all bases are covered, all styles, all angles, grooves and melodies. Lenny has his interests outside of music - acting, interior design and fashion - but its musically where Lenny Kravitz ultimately excels. He's a multi-instrumentalist capable of churning out consistent songs and albums of exceptional quality that will stand the test of time for years and decades to come.

And finally, we return to the beginning...

There is one key feature that remains through all the work of Lenny Kravitz. It's a message that he started with three decades before and a message that he has held onto ever since. It's a mantra he has lived his life by and communicated directly to his millions of fans around the world. It's a simple phrase, one he wrote on a wall and drew inspiration from, and one that has remained as his very core value ever since.

Let Love Rule.

Discography:

Albums:

Let Love Rule
Released: September 6, 1989
Label: Virgin
Formats: LP, cassette, CD, digital download

Mama Said
Released: April 2, 1991
Label: Virgin
Formats: LP, cassette, CD, digital download

Are You Gonna Go My Way
Released: March 9, 1993
Label: Virgin
Formats: LP, cassette, CD, digital download

Circus
Released: September 12, 1995
Label: Virgin
Formats: LP, cassette, CD, digital download

5
Released: May 12, 1998
Label: Virgin
Formats: LP, cassette, CD, digital download

Lenny
Released: October 30, 2001
Label: Virgin
Formats: CD, digital download

Baptism
Released: May 17, 2004
Label: Virgin
Formats: CD, digital download

It Is Time for a Love Revolution
Released: February 5, 2008
Label: Virgin
Formats: CD, digital download

Black and White America
Released: August 30, 2011
Label: Roadrunner/Atlantic
Formats: CD, digital download

Strut
Released: September 19, 2014
Label: Roxie Records/Kobalt Label Services
Formats: CD, digital download

Raise Vibration
Released: September 7, 2018
Label: Roxie Records/BMG

Compilations

Greatest Hits
Released: October 24, 2000
Label: Virgin
Formats: CD, digital download, CD/DVD

BOX SETS
Let Love Rule / Mama Said
Released: October 22, 2001
Format: CD box set

Let Love Rule / Mama Said / Are You Gonna Go My Way
Released: October 7, 2002

5 / Lenny
Released: September 15, 2003
Format: CD box set

Lenny / Baptism
Released: 2004
Formats: CD box set
EP's
1994: Spinning Around Over You
1995: Is There Any Love in the World?

Singles

1989
Let Love Rule

1990
I Build This Garden for Us
Be
Mr. Cab Driver
Does Anybody Out There Even Care

1991
Always on the Run
It Ain't Over 'til It's Over
Fields of Joy
Stand by My Woman
What the Fuck Are We Saying?
Stop Draggin' Around
What Goes Around Comes Around

1993
Are You Gonna Go My Way
Believe
Heaven Help
Spinning Around Over You (soundtrack)
Is There Any Love in Your Heart

1994
Deuce (Kiss My Ass: Classic Kiss Regrooved)

1995
Rock and Roll Is Dead
Circus

1996
Can't Get You Off My Mind
The Resurrection

1998
If You Can't Say No
Thinking of You
I Belong to You
Fly Away

1999
American Woman (Austin Powers: The Spy Who Shagged Me
soundtrack)
Black Velveteen

2000
Again

2001
Dig In

2002
Stillness of Heart
Believe in Me
If I Could Fall in Love
Yesterday Is Gone (My Dear Kay)

2004
Show Me Your Soul (Bad Boys II soundtrack)
Where Are We Runnin'?
California
Storm (with Jay-Z)

2005
Calling All Angels
Lady
Breathe (Non-album single)

2007
Bring It On
I'll Be Waiting

2008
Love Love Love
Dancin' Til Dawn

2011
Come On Get It
Stand
Rock Star City Life
Black and White America
Push

2012
Superlove

2014
The Chamber
Strut
Sex
New York City
Dirty White Boots

2015
The Pleasure and the Pain

2018
It's Enough!
Low
Music Videos
Let Love Rule (Version 1)

Be
Let Love Rule (version 2)
I Build This Garden for Us
Mr. Cab Driver
Always on the Run
It Ain't Over 'til It's Over
Stand by My Woman
Stop Draggin' Around (live)
Are You Gonna Go My Way
Believe
Heaven Help
Is There Any Love in Your Heart
Spinning Around Over You
Rock and Roll Is Dead
Circus (version 1)
Circus (version 2)
Can't Get You Off My Mind (version 1)
Can't Get You Off My Mind (version 2)
If You Can't Say No
Thinking of You
I Belong to You
Fly Away
American Woman
Black Velvetee
Again
Dig In
Stillness of Heart
Believe in Me
If I Could Fall in Love
Yesterday Is Gone (My Dear Kay)
Where Are We Runnin'?
California
Storm (remix)
Lady
Calling All Angels
I'll Be Waiting
Love Love Love
Dancin' Til Dawn

Let Love Rule (remix)
Come On Get It
Stand
Push
Dream
The Chamber
New York City
Sex
The Pleasure and the Pain
It's Enough
Low

About the Author

Growing up through the 1980s James was surrounded by the Pop hits of the day and soon became fascinated with the Pop stars and Musicians that played through the TV and Radio. Here he started searching for something more satisfying and moved through to soul music, jazz, and rhythm and blues. It was Funk however that really got James's attention and from here he never looked back. James Brown, Sly and the Family Stone, Parliament and Prince all captured this perfectly. James loved the way that these groups and individuals brought together a strong melody, chord progressions, rhythmic groove of a bass line and drums. All these factors were then for the first time brought to the foreground. Funk was found and once discovered, James was hooked. James started writing extensively on Prince through various platforms and it wasn't long before he had amassed a significant stockpile of material worthy of a Biography. Over the years James has collected an enviable catalogue of Prince Vinyl Records, CDs, Tapes, Cassette, DVDs and Memorabilia. The Biography was finally completed in 2018, and has been nominated for the 2019 Association for Recorded Sound Collections Awards for Excellence in Historical Recorded Sound Research.

James is delighted to have joined New Haven Publishing and has added to his music icon series, aptly titled The Life The Genius The Legend, with Lenny Kravitz (releases April 29 2019) and Madonna (releases August 30th 2019)

Prince Rogers Nelson.

Guitarist, Drummer, Bass Player, Pianist, Keyboardist, Song Writer, Producer, programmer, Arranger, Vocalist, Business entrepreneur, Actor, Director, Dancer, Choreographer.

James Court has been an avid collector, writer and follower of Prince and his work for more than thirty years. Upon Prince's death in April 2016, James set about the colossal task of revealing every part of this fascinating ever-changing musician, leaving no stone unturned. The Biography tackles the issue's that plagued the Superstar, his fight for Musical freedom and his constant need to write record and perform without restriction or filter.

Often described as the greatest Musician of his generation Prince remained at the very top of the game, a multi-instrumentalist with the ability to write cutting edge songs at will, his talent ability and influence were simply unmatched.

The results make this the most comprehensive, detailed and exhaustingly accurate depiction of one of the most popular, misunderstood and illusive musicians in modern day music....

ISBN 9781949515039
Released November 1st 2018

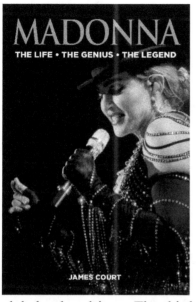

If there is any female artist that warrants the title of 'Queen of Pop' its Madonna. She remains the biggest selling female recording artist on the planet, and undoubtedly one of the greatest living pop stars. Madonna still continues to intelligently reinvent herself with each pioneering album and she has consistently regenerating her music and her image. She has transcended the world of pop for decades to become a true music legend and a global cultural icon. The third book by James Court in The Life The Genius The Legend series, follows every part of Madonna's incredible career in real time. Covering every album, every film and each highlight on the most ground breaking and defining female pop stars the music world has seen. Madonna remains completely unique and unchallenged in her longevity and accomplishments in Music, following her extraordinary career through to 2019. This is her definitive story...

ISBN: 9781912587209
Releases August 30th 2019

CPSIA information can be obtained
at www.ICGtesting.com
Printed in the USA
BVHW040558201020
R11341000001B/R113410PG591032BVX13B/4

9 781912 587186